CINEMATIC SAVIOR

Hollywood's Making of the American Christ

STEPHENSON HUMPHRIES-BROOKS

PRAEGER

Westport, Connecticut
London

Library of Congress Cataloging-in-Publication Data

Humphries-Brooks, Stephenson.
  Cinematic savior : Hollywood's making of the American Christ /
Stephenson Humphries-Brooks.
       p.   cm.
  Includes bibliographical references and index.
  ISBN 0–275–98489–3 (alk. paper)
  1. Jesus Christ—In motion pictures.   2. Motion pictures—United States.   I. Title.
  PN1995.9.J4H86 2006
  791.43'651—dc22   2006002723

British Library Cataloguing in Publication Data is available.

Library of Congress Catalog Card Number: 2006002723
ISBN: 0–275–98489–3

First published in 2006

Praeger Publishers, 88 Post Road West, Westport, CT 06881
An imprint of Greenwood Publishing Group, Inc.
www.praeger.com

Printed in the United States of America

The paper used in this book complies with the
Permanent Paper Standard issued by the National
Information Standards Organization (Z39.48–1984).

10 9 8 7 6 5 4 3 2 1

For Lauren and Sharon

CONTENTS

ACKNOWLEDGMENTS

I completed this book while Sharon, my wife, was diagnosed and treated for breast cancer. The cancer also caused a relatively rare neurological disorder, paraneoplasic syndrome. Her recovery has been slow and difficult. This is to say that this book could never have been completed without the kindness and help of many others in our family and community who gave unstintingly of themselves for Sharon's comfort and my support. The following are those who directly helped with the book.

My students at Hamilton College have taught me more than I can ever say about how film effects the religious values of each generation. I have learned more from them about the Cinematic Savior than they from me.

Mary Anne Beavis first recommended that I send a proposal to Praeger Publishers, Greenwood Press.

My editors at Praeger Publishers and Greenwood Press negotiated a series of extensions of publication deadlines during the ups and downs of Sharon's illness and recovery. Eric Levy, my first editor encouraged the early stages of the book, honing its focus. Daniel Harmon oversaw the final production. I appreciate his rapid, accurate, edits and queries almost as much as his genuine humanity.

Victoria Vernon now retired from the comparative literature department at Hamilton College has been my friend, colleague, and mentor for two decades. She was my first reader, second reader, and always my teacher. Most importantly, she held my hand long distance by e-mail and never doubted me even when I doubted my self.

The center of my creative life has for some years been my family. My daughter Lauren has a vast knowledge of film history and a collection of DVDs that grows daily. She is one of the millennial generation who navigates levels of media existence at a blinding speed but with great sensitivity to artistry and spirituality. She can call title, director, and year of a Hollywood film with frightening accuracy. She remembers large sections of dialogue even after one viewing (a talent discovered when Sharon and I heard her reciting scenes of *Lady and the Tramp* when she was two years old). She read and commented on several chapters especially "How Jesus Got a Gun."

Finally, Sharon started me on the road to this book. She encouraged me to work outside the box of traditional New Testament Studies in which I was trained and to venture into film. She gave me the title of my first course in film and religion, "The Celluloid Savior." Even in the depths of her illness she had me read drafts of this manuscript to her and told me that I must persevere. She is my love, my wife, my friend, and now my example of courage, graciousness, and life in the face of death.

All of these I thank with all of my heart. I hope that this book in some small measure expresses my gratitude for their gifts.

INTRODUCTION

Periodically—and with what can by now be considered the appropriate fanfare, hype, and controversy—America receives a new cinematic version of the Jesus story. Between the 1920s and the early years of the twentieth century, there were at least six major Hollywood film productions of the story, to say nothing of a television miniseries. What is surprising is not that there are so many film adaptations of the same story, but that the versions are so different, and that they tell us as much or more about the state of our contemporary culture as they do about universal or eternal truths. What should we make of the vision of Jesus resurrected over an industrialized America, manifestly not located in the Palestine of the first century of the Common Era? Or of a Jesus taking leave of the cross for an imagined series of marriages to three women before returning to the Crucifixion? How can we explain the varieties of representations of Jesus, his disciples, his betrayer, his temptations, and his mission, unless we are willing to recognize the cultural conflicts that have led America to mix the mission of Christ, the mission of Christianity, and the mission of the United States in the world? As an American audience, we are always trying to work out, in viewing these films, our relationship with the Cinematic Savior and our relationship to his particular form of salvation.

On Ash Wednesday, February 25, 2004, Mel Gibson's *The Passion of the Christ* opened in the thick of another great controversy. On the one side, a collection of scholars and critics, some of whom had seen the script, some of whom had seen the film, some of whom had seen both, and some of whom had seen neither, warned of its anti-Semitic potential. On the other side, religious leaders, scholars, and churchmen claimed it to be an authentic, historical, and inspiring dramatization of the Gospel narratives. It was released in over 2,000 theatres: a major production from a mainstream Hollywood actor and director with Academy Awards under his belt.

Similarly, in 1927, Cecil B. DeMille released the first mainstream Hollywood version of the Passion of Jesus, *King of Kings*. Consider the parallels between these two movies. Both focused on the last days of Jesus, although DeMille set his within the slightly broader context of the ministry of Jesus. The movement from the Last Supper to the Ascension takes up the second half of his movie; in Gibson's, we see only the events that span from the Garden of Gethsemane to the Resurrection. Both claimed authenticity and historicity and were directed by men who were well-established Hollywood insiders. Both men are on record as saying that their film was an act of their own faith commitment. Both garnered opposition from religious groups for anti-Semitism. Both claimed a pious set. The very act of movie production, according to each director, became almost a worship experience. Both were hailed by supporters for having produced an important movie at a time of moral and national crises of faith.

These are the obvious parallels. Less obvious is the fact that both movies were produced at critical junctures of American history. *King of Kings* was released at the height of American industrialization, as the Jazz Age was in full swing, and just two years prior to the collapse of Wall Street. *The Passion of the Christ* arrived four years into a new millennium, at what was arguably the height of American power to date. It was also released 2 1/2 years after the World Trade Center attack of 9/11. In the last frames of *King of Kings* Jesus appears resurrected over America, the Christian light of all nations leading forward into an industrialized world. In the last frames of *The Passion of the Christ,* he strides forth from the tomb to the strains of martial music, as an America perfected by suffering. What do these parallels and differences mean?

Jesus in mainstream Hollywood film is a Cinematic Savior created in an American image. That is, he can be seen both as America and as the Savior of America, for on film he serves as the projection of America's self-image. If he is tempted in *The Last Temptation of Christ,* then it is the temptation of America. If he triumphs to resurrection over the peaceful landscape of the American West in *The Greatest Story Ever Told,* then it is the mythic triumph of America over its bloody past and its ascension to a new spirituality.

Despite repeated claims of authenticity, this Cinematic Savior is not bound by traditional images of Jesus, but is primarily a creation of and contributor to a visual tradition representing America to itself. Hollywood film, which is quintessentially American film, constitutes its own religious culture. It produces its own images, its own story lines, and its own expressions, which refer to the history of American film on the one side and the history of American culture on the other. While it may be the case that, from time to time, church institutions and canonical or legendary Christian texts have exercised an enlivening influence on these representations of Jesus, their traditions are not primary within the films themselves. Rather a special repertoire of plots, characterizations, settings, music, and cinematic techniques, developed in American film, become the prime means of expression in these artistic works and make up the language of imagery in which they are presented. The Cinematic Savior is the American filmic Christ. He tells us who we are and where we are going. Therefore, each new release of a mainstream Hollywood film about Jesus becomes a battlefront for America's culture wars.

Of course, the culture wars didn't yet appear to exist on the hot Kentucky night when my parents took me to a drive-in to see *The Ten Commandments*. Drive-ins were family entertainment in the late 1950s. I was about five years old, and they thought I would go to sleep in the back seat of the Chevy so they could enjoy the movie. Much to my parents' surprise, I stayed awake through the whole epic. I watched, fascinated, while the characters I had been told about in Sunday school became as real as the Lone Ranger and Superman. And afterwards, I never thought of Moses without thinking of Charlton Heston parting the waters of the Red Sea while the chariots of Yul Brenner bore down upon him.

I continued to enjoy biblical and religious films throughout my life. *Ben-Hur* and *The Greatest Story Ever Told* were released when I was in grade school. I wasn't allowed to see *The Greatest Story Ever Told* because Jesus' face was shown on screen and my parents thought it would unduly influence my own developing conception of Jesus. The album and stage productions of *Jesus Christ Superstar* galvanized theological discussions with my friends in high school.

Nevertheless, when I began teaching "The New Testament" and "Jesus and the Gospels" at Hamilton College in New York State, I was surprised at how much and how fast I would be learning. When Martin Scorsese released *The Last Temptation of Christ* in 1988, it created a major buzz among my students. They wanted to know if the movie was accurate, possible, or fictional. Eight years of graduate education had not prepared me for what the average college student brings to the study of Jesus. Those of my students who prided themselves on having ignored their religious upbringing still possessed firm opinions about who Jesus was and what his life meant. But most of what I heard came from the movies, not the Bible. Even those students who came from biblically informed backgrounds possessed similar opinions. My students believed in a Cinematic Savior.

Where, I wondered, had I been? How has Hollywood replaced the church as the producer of Jesus' image in our imaginations and our faith? Unlike the church, Hollywood is not bound to canonical traditions of who Jesus is or where he is leading. Instead, this Christ can be refashioned in direct response to the current artistic and market situations. He exists as one great mythological character alongside a whole pantheon of other Hollywood heroes. As the character with whom America identifies itself, he bears incredible persuasive weight, a fact appreciated by Hollywood from DeMille onward. Therefore, by looking at "Jesus" in film, we can gain insight into what the Cinematic Savior can teach us about what is distinctive in American culture. We can trace the changes in America's religion, theology, and, most importantly, self-concept by a careful analysis of the Hollywood Jesus movies. As Hollywood regularly shows us its continually variable Cinematic Savior, it presents to us a renewable American Christ. Since in one way or another Hollywood produces or influences visual representation in an overwhelming amount of television and movies worldwide, the American religious culture of film is fast becoming a world culture. Our mythology dominates the global market.

People take sides on these movies. The Cinematic Savior and his continuing development show that the image of Jesus bears witness to who we are and where we are going. This image can no longer be controlled by official religion in the form of the church (as if it ever could). At the crossroads of the millennium, claims are being made on all sides as to the "true" or the "historical" or the "coming" Jesus. But as he continues to change, we need to understand better why and how his story remains so important to us.

Perhaps chastened by exposure to a generation of students who had already formed an image of the Cinematic Savior by the time they arrived on campus, I began to incorporate the study of film representations of Jesus into my courses. I'm glad I did, for I have continued to learn much from the films and from the students, and have been fascinated by the way in which the genre of the Jesus film has developed over time.

The following chapters are a result of that study and seek to explain how Jesus, as a specifically Cinematic Savior, has changed from DeMille's *King of Kings* to Gibson's *The Passion of the Christ* in order to bring the American Christ into clear relief. *The Passion of the Christ*, far from presenting a brand new and now definitive Jesus, uses the whole history of Hollywood film to produce its Cinematic Savior and present us with a new American Christ. I have chosen to trace the influences on *The Passion of the Christ* almost exclusively from the five major Hollywood productions of Jesus movies that precede it: *King of Kings* (1927), *King of Kings* (1961), *The Greatest Story Ever Told* (1965), *Jesus Christ Superstar* (1973), and *The Last Temptation of Christ* (1989).

I have diverged from this trajectory at only two points. First, I will be examining the significance of *Jesus of Nazareth*, the first television miniseries, which appeared in 1976—after *Jesus Christ Superstar* and before *The Last Temptation of Christ*. Its influence on the American Christ and on subsequent Cinematic Saviors, including *The Passion of the Christ*, was so important that it requires a careful analysis. We should keep in mind that Franco Zeffirelli, the director of *Jesus of Nazareth*, also directed Gibson in *Hamlet*. After this first divergence, and in order to understand the characterization of Jesus as an American action hero in *The Passion of the Christ*, I look at the hybridization of elements of the Jesus story with conventional American heroes in other genres in Chapter 7: "How Jesus Got a Gun."

Earlier analyses of Jesus movies have chosen to center on their plot and dialogue as primary bearers of meaning and theology. Most previous interpreters also look at these movies through comparison with the canonical Gospels of Matthew, Mark, Luke, and John, and with church teaching. While I have learned much from such studies (please see the list in "Works Consulted") this is not the approach taken here.

Unlike text, film conveys its meaning by direct visual representation. The perspective of the camera is the only perspective provided the viewer. Unlike stage productions, where an individual's seat in a theatre may change his or her view of the action, in a two-dimensional movie we have only one view. This means that film is, on the one hand, highly visual, flat, and controlling. On the other hand, film prompts our imagination through its sounds and images, and possible interpretations are multiplied as compared to reading texts. Moreover the film experience is sequential and cumulative. Many of the visual impressions we receive are subliminal and/or residual. The symbolic weight of the visual is heavy although no direct interpretation of the symbols is given in the film to the viewer. So, how shall we understand it when in *King of Kings* (1927) the temple curtain is split in two, the insignia of the menorah bursts into flame, and we see a cross of light ascending skyward? Why are Herod Antipas, Herodias, and Salome represented as Arabs in *King of Kings* (1961)? When *The Passion of the Christ* shows us a brutal scourging of Jesus for

12 minutes on screen, what are we to make of the eroticization of the violence thus depicted?

Rather than historical authenticity, or the real Christ, what is at stake for these movies is America's sense of itself—its ideals, its theology, its mythology, and its salvation. We must remember that *King of Kings* (1927) ends with Christ ascending over a peaceful, productive, industrial cityscape. He is the future of America. *The Passion of the Christ* ends with the action hero Christ who, having suffered sadistic torture on screen, strides triumphantly from the tomb. What do these Christs and all those in between say about America?

Certain motifs emerge and are repeated in the filmic vocabulary of the Cinematic Savior. Mary Magdalene poses the temptation of sex to Jesus; Judas, Satan, and Jewish officials manifest the problems of wealth, avarice, and greed; foreign imperialism is linked with sadism in Roman officials; and often the ethnic identification implied by the casting of Jesus, the disciple band, and others keys the audience in to a certain preferred identity in America. The geography provided by location and camera technique frequently creates a mythic American landscape where Jesus undergoes temptation, suffering, and triumph. A major bridge to this landscape is the musical score of each film. All of these elements interact in a given film to provide the audience with a clear picture of their contemporary America and of the Savior who will deliver them, but who is also one with them.

In this book we establish a new way of looking at Jesus films. Previous discussions of Jesus in film have been dominated by one form or another of adaptation theory, that is, by the question of how a particular film conforms to, expresses, or changes the traditional view of Jesus as represented in the four canonical Gospels and in church traditions. I am more interested in film's power to describe the changing religious culture of mainstream America.

While I do not ignore the notion of the director as an "auteur," I think it is also important to recognize that these films have been created in a smaller culture (usually associated with Hollywood) and then moved to a broader culture (American audiences). I want to expose for the reader the latent elements that the audience might experience but not quite be able to name.

I have found inspiration for this approach in Peter Fraser's *Images of the Passion: The Sacramental Mode in Film*, and Gerald Forshey's *American Religious and Biblical Spectaculars*. Although these works do not trace the Hollywood Jesus movie as a genre in itself, both authors describe film as a religiously laden culture in its own right. In addition, Stephen Prothero's

American Jesus: How the Son of God Became a National Icon was a significant catalyst for my own thinking. His book provides the cultural history into which the Cinematic Savior may be fitted.[1]

All of the major films discussed in this work are now available on videocassette and/or DVD, as are the considerable number of other movies more briefly referred to in the book. This is a fascinating circumstance, unforeseeable at the time when the earliest of the Jesus films were released, and it makes me reflect on the current moment. In the past a film appeared once in major release in movie theatres. For most audience members repeated showings would not be available except for second runs at some theatres and drive-ins. Now, to the contrary, these movies are truly "icons" in the traditional religious sense of the term. They are repeatedly available in the home as objects of study, edification, and for some, something akin to worship. The power of the Cinematic Savior has become a part of the eternal media stream generated by Hollywood. This makes careful analysis and understanding all the more important in our times, beset as they are by a variety of appeals to the icon of Jesus.

I invite readers, therefore, to make use of the current opportunities to view the films themselves as they follow the argument of the ensuing chapters. The films and the text may play off against each other in unforeseeable ways and inspire the reader/viewer to reflect on the changing meanings of the Jesus story in the Hollywood films of the twentieth and twenty-first centuries and the changing culture in which we locate ourselves as Americans.

1

LOVE AND BETRAYAL:
MAGDALENE, JUDAS, AND JESUS

THE FIRST MAKING OF THE AMERICAN CHRIST

King of Kings begins Hollywood's making of the American Christ, the Cinematic Savior. Previous silent films, most notably D. W. Griffith's *Intolerance* (1916), had depicted Jesus on screen, but Cecil B. DeMille was the first maker of a truly American Christ. The influence of *King of Kings* at the levels of cinematography, film technique, point of view, and most importantly, mythmaking, cannot be overestimated. *King of Kings* moves Christ's image out of church control and into the realm of American popular culture as never before. Christ becomes a major player in the media, and neither the church nor Hollywood would be the same after 1927.

King of Kings stands at the beginning of DeMille's contribution to the development of the biblical spectacular. Silent film depended fundamentally on visual images for its effects, and since we are schooled in the "talkies," the film may appear melodramatic or overdone to us today. For example, DeMille makes extensive use of titles to tell the viewer how to see the movie (compare to the sparse use of titles in Buster Keaton's *Sherlock Jr.* [1924]). In his visual images, however, DeMille expresses dramatic sensitivity and a mythic consciousness that will later explode full force in *The Ten Commandments* (1956).

The movie creates much of its dramatic force by the love triangle of Magdalene, Jesus, and Judas. The triangle is fictitious, a contribution of the imagination of the moviemaker. While DeMille claims in his opening statement that these events happened, those that are key to the development of the drama do not occur in the Gospels. In Mark, Matthew, and John, Magdalene appears for the first time at the foot of the cross. Only Luke records her as "the one out of whom seven demons were cast."

No Gospels consider her a prostitute. Her characterization as such develops in later Christian legend. DeMille adds his own creative development of the tradition of a love interest in the Gospel story by making Magdalene a "courtesan" and lover of Judas.

Judas, likewise, receives little attention in the Gospels—he is simply the betrayer. Mark, Matthew, and John indicate that his motivation is greed. Luke and John state that Satan entered him. None report that he is a disappointed seeker of political power through Jesus. DeMille begins the Hollywood tradition of examining the motives of Judas. Judas will be refashioned repeatedly in each succeeding Jesus movie.

The movie follows Matthew in showing Judas's suicide, and the scene becomes a favorite for subsequent films. DeMille shows the developing despair and even insanity that lead to Judas's suicide. He develops the Matthean element of making Judas's tragic death parallel to Jesus' salvific one. The movie dramatizes and elevates the great tension between Judas's life and Jesus' for the audience. Why couldn't Jesus save Judas? Because Judas refused!

THE MODERN FIFTH GOSPEL

Furthermore, *King of Kings* contains creative additions to plot and characterization that produce what is essentially a new story, despite DeMille's own claim to accuracy. His claim of historicity is strongest in the opening frames, where the movie asserts an authoritative position for the director:

> Events portrayed by this picture occurred in Palestine nineteen centuries ago, when the Jews were under the complete subjection of Rome—even their own High Priest being appointed by the Roman procurator.

Now, the movie states, you will know the truth about Jesus. *King of Kings* purports to tell history while erecting it. DeMille also states clearly the intention of the movie to proselytize for Jesus' message, "May this portrayal play a reverent part in the spirit of that great command. . ."

The combination of pseudo-historical authority with a modern Protestant desire to convert governs DeMille's movie. In this representation canonical Gospel or gospel-like scenes do occur. But they are components of a modern fifth gospel constructed by the movie. Jesus' healing ministry takes place almost exclusively in one scene in his own house, in Galilee.

Lazarus is raised, apparently on the outskirts of Jerusalem. Jesus cleanses the temple. There is no triumphal entry, but the people sing hosannas and call for his coronation as king accompanied by the Hallelujah Chorus. In a departure from Gospel order he is here tempted by Satan after the cleansing of the temple. He is betrayed. He celebrates the Last Supper. Tried by Pilate, he is condemned for sedition. Crucified, he rises. He appears first to Magdalene and then to the eleven. In these scenes, the movie plot closely approximates the plot of the Gospels, but it departs from them in specific details.

King of Kings weaves together quotations derived directly from the King James Version of the Bible. This technique, in a medium that is partly written and partly visual, lends particular authority and "authenticity" to the movie. So much is this the case that when we read fictitious dialogue, it occurs in the cadences of scripture. Creation is indistinguishable from tradition. DeMille knows his audience well. He provides a plausible scenario for an audience that knows scripture. Given the general education in Bible studies in church and school in 1927, he can rely on his audience to make the connection, whereas current general audiences have a more difficult time appreciating the biblical associations that the movie demands. The director further enhances biblical and pious associations by using as many as 276 paintings from church art as the basis for his sets.[1]

Not only plot and characterization, but the overall landscape of the movie unify its message. The cast is homogenous; only one African appears. The remainder, with only two notable exceptions, Caiaphas and Judas, are recognizably white Americans in biblical costume.

Characterization bleeds over into the political message of the movie. Conflicts are between the rich and a rising middle class. Unlike the Gospel stories of Jesus, in the film there is almost no depiction of the truly poor. Enter the American story of the downtrodden, pious common man. Jesus, his disciples, and his mother Mary are presented consistently as pious homeowners not unlike the movie's intended audience. The movie avoids any suggestion of the homelessness of Jesus as depicted in the Gospels. He moves from his house to Jerusalem. He carries on no outdoor ministry to the poor. He heals beautiful, clean, children and women, all represented throughout the course of the film as young and Anglo. *King of Kings* establishes within its first 45 minutes the special relationship of healing between Jesus as the Light of the World and these two groups. No lepers and no vilely oppressed or impoverished people appear. Our Savior is one of us, says the movie: white, male, and Protestant.

Protestant church music of the early 1900s dominates the soundtrack of the movie. Since a 1927 movie audience would be predominantly white,

Protestant, and comparatively liberal, the soundtrack provides a bridge to make Jesus utterly familiar and American. From this perspective, there is predictably no controversial teaching. Jesus is a pious, middle-class, middle-aged man, a miraculous leader, but not a threat to the established social or political order. His kingdom is not of this world. His threat is to the individual sins of lust, greed, hypocrisy, and overweening political power.

The landscape and settings of the movie provide major bridges from the ancient to the modern world. The sets of the temple and Pilate's throne are high modern. Pilate's throne room clearly shows the influence of art deco style. Even the stylized armor of the Roman soldiers shows similar modern influence. In these particulars of landscape and design, the movie provides the mythic bridge between the audience's time and the ancient time of Jesus. It assaults the decadence of the new and too progressive modern order.

As the silent medium demands, the movie is oriented towards dramatic action. Long speeches provide little visual interest. Totally absent is any of Jesus' familiar teaching. He tells no parables, gives no commandments. He is not a preacher nor a revealer of divine speech. He performs miracles of healing and raising the dead in naturalistic scenes. He shows himself to be God, or so we think, by means of his penetrating gaze.

THE LOVE TRIANGLE

In a cinematic stroke, the "love" triangle between Jesus, Judas, and Magdalene, though potentially controversial, was to prove successful dramatically in *King of Kings*. In its resolution the spiritual nature of Jesus' love wins out over other possibly erotic viewpoints. Later movies, most notably *The Last Temptation of Christ*, return to the same dramatic theme. In the case of *The Last Temptation of Christ*, the resolutions become quite controversial.

Magdalene becomes the model for faith in *King of Kings*, although her introduction would not make us suppose so. The opening scene of the movie depicts her as a "courtesan," a high-priced party girl who controls the men around her by her beauty and will. She lives a luxurious life of sexual freedom at the expense of aristocratic suitors.

More than oriental in its splendor, Magdalene's boudoir comes complete with exotic animals. Scantily clad, she evokes Hollywood in its glamour and glitz. She is young, lovely, and desirable, surrounded only by men. She has no regard for "God or man." She represents free, sexual, feminine power. She is aristocratic, sinful, and licentious. She is an extreme type of American decadence.

Her very extremity strongly signifies for the audience an excessive pagan lifestyle. The American and biblical spectacular steadily exhibits pagans in this way for American audiences, and DeMille is a prime author of this representation (see for example the highly eroticized presentations in *The Sign of the Cross* [1932]). Such strong depiction of the pagan against the Christian allows Hollywood to explore sexual and sadomasochistic themes even after the adoption of the production code.[2] DeMille, as his entire career demonstrates, used sex, sadism, and melodrama as the primary ingredients of biblical spectacular.

The extremity of Magdalene's initial representation also highlights the threatening secular world of America in opposition to Protestant piety. By dwelling on the visual opulence of her boudoir, the scene suggests that Magdalene and Judas, who has been a member of her entourage, are aristocrats, and perhaps social climbers. They are the beautiful people. Thus, Magdalene's later conversion can be interpreted as the reformation of secular America.

This opening scene goes on to reveal an unusual love triangle, for it introduces the plot element of a contest between Magdalene and Jesus for Judas's devotion. Magdalene discovers that Judas, one of her suitors, has gone after Jesus, a carpenter, healer, and magician who can raise the dead. Magdalene assumes that there is a homosexual affair between Judas and Jesus. In a chariot drawn by zebras that was the gift of the King of Nubia, she sets off for Jesus' house.

Half naked and defiant, Magdalene searches out Jesus and confronts him over Judas. He responds to the confrontation with a penetrating gaze that convicts her of sin. Throughout the movie his gaze is a sign of divine, spiritual, miraculous power standing in contrast to the furtive looks of the fleshly, human world. In an act of spiritual healing, Jesus casts seven female demons out from Magdalene. They are identified by titles as the seven deadly sins of lust, greed, pride, gluttony, indolence, envy, and anger. While this element draws on a brief reference to Magdalene in the Gospel of Luke, the movie visually links her to the deadly sins of humanity.

Placing lust first, *King of Kings* prioritizes the tie between sin and sexuality. By choosing Magdalene as the symbol for universal sinfulness and by making each demon a wanton female, the film constructs Woman as the universal symbol of the dark, fleshly sins of humanity. American film foregrounds the tie between Woman and evil in the creation of American mythology. In addition, the sins of greed and pride are prioritized for the viewer by longer screen time. These three sins—lust, greed, and pride—are the dominant concerns of *King of Kings*. Jesus may die for all the sins of the world, but dramatically the viewer focuses on only these three.

Magdalene covers herself. Through the remainder of the movie she will be depicted as a younger version of Mary, the mother of Jesus. She is the sinner become Madonna. Magdalene's sexuality will remain, but sublimated visually to a higher, spiritual key.

In this scene Jesus converts Magdalene's sexual love to spiritual devotion. The movie depicts this devotion as a spiritual vision. Her devotion is robust, evangelistic fervor, rather than licentious behavior. Nevertheless, her screen energy displays an underlying, heaving sensuality despite the shifts in her outward dress and self-presentation. From this point forward her story is one of success. She will follow Jesus to the cross and to the tomb. She becomes the image of faith. Magdalene ends the movie by discovering the resurrected Jesus at his tomb. Her success in faith is rewarded by this beatific vision in the only scene shot in color in an otherwise black and white film.

The second member of the dramatic love triangle is Judas. We meet him at the house of Jesus as "the ambitious, who joined the disciples in the belief that Jesus would be the nation's King and reward him with honor and high office." By this note the narrator of the movie, identified earlier as DeMille himself, introduces the motivation for Judas, who is wealthy, young, handsome, and clean-shaven. He misunderstands Jesus and in his quest to profit by him, he sells Jesus out.

This characterization of Judas uses physical beauty and youth to depict evil intention. A later scene presents Satan in the same way. The story of Judas is a tragedy contained within the redemptive plot of Jesus' life. Joseph Schildkraut, who plays Judas, is one of two Jewish actors cast in a principle part. The other is Rudolph Schildkraut, his father, cast as Caiaphas. They are visually clearly distinguished from Jesus and the disciple band. The visual representation and casting of Judas, then, associates youth, beauty, wealth, and Jewishness with evil intention in the passion of Jesus.

Jesus, the third member of the triangle, first appears just prior to the arrival of Magdalene. A blind girl comes to Jesus for healing, with the help of Mark, the future Evangelist, whose crippled leg Jesus had healed. (The Gospels lack any information about Mark. Here, he is brilliant American screen fiction.)

Mary, the mother, calls her son to tend to the child, and appears in dress strongly parallel to the habits worn by ordered sisters. She is an older, chaste, and respectable version of Magdalene. She weaves in the house. Thus, proper femaleness is associated with proper dress and domesticity. She is also observing the Sabbath, ceasing her work at sundown.

In a brilliant cinematographic move, the film reveals Jesus to us through the slowly opened eyes of the blind child. "I begin to see the light," the child says. This is the theological theme of the film. Jesus appears to her as to us in a halo of light. He will be backlit throughout the film, lending to his ethereal otherness and designating him as the Light. This healing, not found in the Gospels, shows the compassion of Jesus. He hugs the child to him as he does Magdalene.

The creative and authoritative theological moment is now reinforced for the viewer as the camera's eye. Since film depends for its effect on the integration of lighting in constructing visual representation, then in its lighting *King of Kings* excels at communicating its theological perspective consistently. The camera may be relied upon to expose the divine nature of Jesus. He constantly is suffused by halo lighting from above. He is the Light of the World in every appearance.

All of the disciples except Judas and Peter are introduced in an almost cursory manner. Most later films follow the same tendency, foreshadowed in the Gospels, which give the clearest characterization to Judas and Peter. In the movie Judas's ambition motivates him to follow Jesus. He believes that Jesus will reward him with high political office and power. Peter, on the other hand, is an ordinary fisherman of simple faith. The contrast between the two sets—the young and ambitious upper class against the stable working man—is another element typical to American myth.

In Jesus' house, the drama for Jesus' life has been set in motion. Jesus saves Magdalene to personal cleanness, wholeness, and respectability. Judas refuses to see and hear Jesus. He maintains an erroneous belief that Jesus will give him political power. Jesus now goes out into the world.

CAIAPHAS THE PERSONAL ANTAGONIST OF JESUS

Jesus, the Light of the World, comes as a miracle worker and divine presence who will heal and save the low of the earth, the sick, the simple, women and children, through faith. The triangle—Jesus, Magdalene, and Judas—brackets the movie and gives it its unity. The dramatic tension between the three resolves only in the Crucifixion and Resurrection scenes.

Before turning to those climactic scenes, however, let us discuss briefly a fourth major character in the film. The high priest, Caiaphas, becomes the agent responsible for Jesus' death. The spies of the high priest are introduced early in the episode at Jesus' house. They watch to entrap him. They provide a sinister tie to Caiaphas himself, who appears immediately following the exorcism of Magdalene. He is a hypocrite, appointed by the

Roman procurator. From this point onward he will reappear strategically as the personal antagonist of Jesus who personally sees that Jesus dies. His council room shows opulence equal to Magdalene's boudoir, except it is a powerful male's room devoid of sexual allusions. Caiaphas himself is the callous, ruthless embodiment of evil.

DeMille mutes Caiaphas's association with Judaism in the plot and titles of the film. The term Jew, or "the Jews" prominent in John's Gospel occurs only on the sign over the cross. The opposition to Jesus comes only from a corrupt high priest and his henchmen. So careful is this editorial shaping that it is Caiaphas in the trial before Pilate who demands crucifixion in a whispered suggestion in Pilate's ear, "If thou, imperial Pilate, wouldst wash thy hands of this Man's death, let it be upon me—and me alone."

On the surface, Jesus' death does not come about through the ill will of the Jewish people. The early Christian view of Jews as "Christ Killers" resulted in the pogroms and ghettoization established frequently by state law in the West. It will contribute to the acceptability of Nazi atrocities in Germany only a few years after the release of the movie. In the movie's interpretation, however, Caiaphas opposes his own will to the will of God. His tragic flaw is the universal drive to greed and pride rooted in religious and political power. This new interpretation in a popular medium at a propitious historical moment establishes a trajectory of interpretation for future Jesus films.

As opposed to this clear narrative interpretation, which might suggest an absence of anti-Semitism, visual characterization in King of Kings must also be considered. As noted above, only Judas and Caiaphas are portrayed by Jewish actors. Rudolph Shildkraut (Caiaphas) was noted for stage portrayals of Shylock.[3] Joseph (Judas) will later portray Nicodemus in The Greatest Story Ever Told (1965). In the image vocabulary of King of Kings, the latent message is that Jesus and his disciples are white, Anglo-Saxon, American Protestants who share the values of hardworking pious American Protestants. Their opponents and crucifiers are rich and Jewish. In the scene of condemnation before the mob, Caiaphas's hair is noticeably reminiscent of the forelocks worn by traditional orthodox Jewish men.

Ultimately, King of Kings tends to assimilate the character of Caiaphas into the caricature of "the greedy Jew" familiar to an American audience from Medieval and Reformation traditions. An American audience may "know" that Jesus, his mother, and his disciples are Jewish, but when mainstream film casts him and depicts him as visually and ethnically Anglo-American, the viewers see him as American. In contrast, his opponents are visually and ethnically Jewish. The message becomes clear; America's preferred vision of itself and its Christ still holds latent, if not overt, anti-Semitic tones.

THE RESOLUTION OF THE TRIANGLE

The climax of *King of Kings* is in the Crucifixion and Resurrection of Jesus. These two scenes provide the tragic conclusion to Judas's life and the redemptive beginning of Jesus' life beyond the normal confines of history. *King of Kings* by full use of the motion picture medium shapes the mythology and theology of America.

The scene shifts between the preparations for Crucifixion and Judas's preparations for suicide. Roman soldiers drive in the nails, although we never see the flesh torn. Judas apparently can see the Crucifixion from another hill. A deep valley separates his death scene from Jesus'. This setting is a bold statement about God's relationship to each. The chasm evokes images of the division between heaven and hell (see for example the parable of the rich man and Lazarus in Luke 16:19–29).

The Gospel of Matthew is the only Gospel to recount the suicide of Judas. While Matthew allows for an interpretation of the death of Judas as parallel to the death of Jesus, DeMille's movie version makes this comparison visually riveting. In Matthew, the more natural comparison is between Judas's suicide and Peter's denial of Jesus. Peter never denies Jesus in *King of Kings*. He is not a dramatic focus of the movie. Instead the dramatic climax is constructed by the deaths of Judas and Jesus. The death of Judas is tragic, representing the depths of human sin and psychosis. The death of Jesus is pure and divinely salvific. Jesus is hung on the cross by nails. Judas wraps the cord, which was the belt of Jesus' robe in the earlier scene of mockery, around his own throat and hangs himself. Judas's sin is one of greed, political ambition, and faithlessness. The slow counting of thirty pieces of silver in the betrayal scene cements the association of Judas, Caiaphas, and their Jewishness with money and betrayal.

The dramatic climax of the movie depends in large measure on the scene of the Crucifixion in Matthew. A cataclysm in the heavens and earth is depicted. Darkness and whirlwind descend in divine judgment.

As in Luke, Jesus dies calmly: "Father, into thy hands I commend my spirit." But as Jesus dies, Judas simultaneously hangs himself. The movie takes the death of Judas, clearly separated in Matthew (27:3–5) from the Crucifixion (27:32–54), and makes them dramatically parallel. The judgment against Judas is confirmed by the earth swallowing him as if to hell. This is Hollywood mythmaking at its best.

Intercut with these scenes that juxtapose Jesus and Judas are the faithful presence of the women and the jeering presence of the high priest and his henchmen. The two Marys watch from the foot of the cross along with a third woman. Absent is any sense of jeering by the crowds generally, as we find in several of the Gospels. *King of Kings* consistently focuses on Caiaphas and a few bad priests as the effective cause of Jesus' death.

Jesus, according to Christian artistic tradition now transferred to the screen, is crucified differently from the two thieves. He is only nailed to the crossbeam; they are tied at the arms. This marks his suffering as special and perhaps more painful. *King of Kings* adopts Luke's interpretation of the death of these two by designating them as criminals. Matthew and Mark use a Greek word meaning "bandit," or "revolutionary." For *King of Kings* Jesus is not to be associated with revolutionaries, thereby muting any understanding of his mission as involving political action or resistance. His death is a tragic blunder.

The Gospels themselves give few details about the Crucifixion. Only John mentions the specific scars on the hands, feet, and sides. Luke's scene seems to dominate the interpretation of the movie. Only Luke contains the dialogue, depicted here, between Jesus and the criminals, one of whom begs to be remembered by Jesus.

The theology of Jesus' death in this movie comes closest to Luke. The personal decision for conversion is emphasized in individual reactions to Jesus' death. Immediately after Judas's death, Magdalene hugs the cross. A soldier stabs Jesus in the side, as if killing Jesus will finally end the disturbance of the earth and heavens. But it is only with the confession of the centurion, "Surely this man was the Son of God," that the winds subside. God is appeased by the personal confession of faith. It is noteworthy that the confession comes from a Roman soldier, indicating pagan (secular) conversion. A crow as a symbol of death and judgment lights upon the cross of the thief who derided Jesus.

The high priest runs to the temple, where he watches the tearing and torching of the veil. This veil separates the Holy of Holies from the Holy Place of the temple in Jerusalem. Behind it the Ark of the Covenant given to Moses on Sinai is located, as *King of Kings* has reminded the audience in an earlier scene. Israel considered this space the most sacred in the temple. Only certain priests at special religious celebrations could enter. It was the space where God was considered to specially visit Israel.

Caiaphas confesses his guilt, "Lord God, Jehovah, visit not thy wrath on thy Israel, I alone am guilty." He is the final tragic character. The movie consistently avoids any overt anti-Semitic reading. It rewrites Matt 27:25 "His blood be upon us and our children's children," uttered by the people. The lone, evil, high priest is responsible, and he repents by saying, "Oh God, give us back the light."

God, however, judges Israel despite Caiaphas's plea. When the temple veil is split by lightning, the menorah on the veil is replaced by a rising cross of light. The cross rises out of the Jewish menorah. Jesus rises from the dead. The film shows that Christianity, a living religion, rises out of Judaism judged because it failed to recognize Jesus as the Light. The symbolism is clear. In this movie, Christianity has displaced Judaism as the religion of God. God has left Israel.

God responds to the Crucifixion by Resurrection. Immediately following the splitting of the veil, there is a fade to black followed by a cut to color, an expensive and experimental process in 1927. The Roman soldiers have fallen asleep. Jesus walks from the tomb bathed in the light. DeMille uses color to suggest that here the divine world breaks into the normal, sinful, historical world of black and white. Thereby he places the Resurrection in a filmic "sacred space."

The tomb scene concentrates on Magdalene. It is the conclusion to her story of regeneration and faithfulness. She is shrouded in the black of mourning. Doves flutter around the tomb, symbols of the Holy Spirit. Jesus approaches as a dove rests upon her arm. There remains a beautiful but now sublime sexuality in her posture and face, a mystical yearning for union with the Christ. Judas has gone to tragic destruction. Magdalene receives the first vision of the resurrected Lord.

The subsequent scene in the upper room establishes the resolution of the story set in motion by the first scene in Magdalene's boudoir. If the first scene represents corrupt America, the final scene represents saved, Christian America. Now Mary the Mother, Magdalene, and the disciples greet Jesus as he appears first as a cross of light and then as himself, through the closed door. While "Abide in Me" plays in the background, Jesus proclaims the Great Commission; as the music shifts to "Rock of Ages," we are promised, "Lo I am with you always," as the face of Jesus ascends over a modern, industrial cityscape.

The resolution of the story of Jesus in *King of Kings* marks the ongoing ideology of Jesus as benevolent guide to an ever-progressing American civilization. By framing the movie with these two scenes—Magdalene's boudoir and the Ascension over America—DeMille gives us visions of the dangerous present and preferred future of America.

KING OF KINGS AND THE FIRST MAKING OF THE AMERICAN CHRIST

An estimated 500 million viewers saw *King of Kings* between its release in 1927 and the release of its remake in 1961. In a public relations coup, DeMille arranged a showing for a group of 1,000 ordered sisters at the newly opened Grauman's Chinese theatre. He aimed to secure popular

Catholic approval after a showing for the Hollywood elite where many left before the end of the movie. *King of Kings* was the third most popular movie of 1927 behind *The Jazz Singer* and *Wings*. *The Jazz Singer*, the first "talkie," beat out *King of Kings* for the Oscar. A review in *Variety* proclaimed that the movie was "providentially presented at a moment when the North American side of the universe appears to have about gone crazy in its ideas and opinions or movements and notions or morals."[4]

In *King of Kings*, Hollywood makes its first American Christ. So much of the film becomes the template for subsequent Jesus movies that we will be able to see its influences straight through to Gibson's *The Passion of the Christ*. A deep mythological structure in the film provides understanding of the deep resonances that this movie holds. The two scenes of Magdalene's boudoir and the upper room frame the movie and provide the mythic polarities of American life resolved by the presence of Jesus as the Light. The transformation of faith that moves Magdalene from lustful courtesan to exemplar of faith underscores the transformation being accomplished by the Christ for individuals and through them for American society generally.

The children, Mary the Mother, Magdalene, and Peter represent the genuineness of simple faith. They are domestic, decent believers. The opposite of this goodness is the corruption of lust, greed, and pride. The defining conflict of the movie, therefore, is between decent middle-class life and the urbane aristocracy of hypocritical modern power in its desire for wealth, political power, and sexual freedom.

These elements shape the myth of *King of Kings*. Jesus comes from God to the world to convict individuals of their sins. He forces a decision for individual moral responsibility. These individual decisions are linked to intimate close-ups of the face of Jesus always suffused by light. Hence, the intimate imaginings of Christian piety are expressed visually over time by the modern electronic medium. The camera lets us see into the process of salvation between Jesus and the convert. In the characterizations of Magdalene, Judas, and Caiaphas we see the way in which his offered salvation is accepted or rejected. He saves from sins of lust, greed, and pride, which are also the sins of America at the end of the Jazz Age. He is crucified by individual ill will, the unfaith of Judas and Caiaphas. He rises again as the Light of the World. Faith is an individual relationship to the Christ. What in the Gospels is a story of cosmic significance becomes one of individual decision. Here we have a perfected moving icon of American Protestant faith.

Within this framework, Pilate remains an undecided character. He is presented with the truth and philosophizes with Jesus about truth. His decision to crucify is really a nondecision, since it is brought about by the conniving of Caiaphas. The presentation of Pilate as a confused and rather powerless ruler, backed visually in his courtroom by a stylized Roman eagle, may well be read as a reference to the secular American state (our Eagle a derivative of Rome's) whose diffidence needs to be converted to the definitive truth of the Christ. Certainly, the conversion of at least one Roman soldier, the centurion at the foot of the cross, symbolically holds hope for the state and with it the nation. Note carefully also that the Crucifixion scene, which contains judgment of Caiaphas's henchmen, the recalcitrant thief, and Judaism itself, shows us no direct judgment of the representatives of Rome. Rome, or rather America, remains an open mission field.

Although it is quite clear, then, that *King of Kings* produces a highly traditional view of Jesus for its audience, the camera's mythic eye, while comfortable with the miraculous intervention of God into the normal world, seems uneasy about the relationship between Jesus and God. Its perception of Jesus seems to be that Jesus is a man specially chosen by God to be the Light. In other scenes we have something like the claim that Jesus and God are one and the same. *King of Kings* cannot settle on either depiction. Jesus also is depicted as an innocent victim or martyr. It remains unclear to what extent he anticipates his own end.

Thus, for all its traditional piety, *King of Kings* is a modern depiction of the American Christ. It contains within its point of view a profound uneasiness with divine intervention into the normal historical world. It may be mythological in the sense of attempting a resolution of good and evil along clear traditional pathways, but it is demythologizing in the modern sense of seeking to remove divine transcendence from direct effect in historical process. It cannot decide if Jesus is God or descended from God.

King of Kings is, however, finally a fully modern Protestant view of Jesus on film. It can depend on a strong mainstream consensus about America and Jesus for the establishment of its reading. This makes the movie's final image most important, because here the preferred direction for the ideal viewer is established. Whether or not miracles still happen, whether or not God still intervenes directly to change the historical process, America, like the disciples, is called to promulgate the message of Jesus as the Light of the World who saves the individual. That message is intimately tied to the social structure and values of householder America. The danger is from sexuality, greed, and pride (the last two represented by the Jew); those forces opposed to family values in America.

In the last frame of the film, it easy to see the influence of Bruce Barton, who served as advisor on the film and who had published to best-seller status *The Man Nobody Knows* four years before (although Barton's desire for a robust, manly, masterful Jesus never really materializes in the characterization of Jesus by H. B. Warner). The promise and the hope of total American and worldwide conversion to the salvation of Jesus as the Light is peaceful prosperity under smokestacks of progressive industry. Jesus as the American Christ embraces industrialization, the modern era. Those who oppose will be judged.

It is easy to see why *Variety* would hail this movie as "providentially presented." Jesus in this movie remains the more passive Christ of nineteenth-century America. The American belief in clearly drawn battle lines between good and evil and the American belief that Christ supports, embodies, and blesses our national values are fully articulated in this movie. DeMille's film begins the film representations, the icons of Hollywood's Cinematic Savior, that later Jesus films will copy and modify to suit their needs. *King of Kings*, even though it will give way to grander spectacle and ever more refined film techniques, continues to define our image of ourselves as Americans and of our Christ. With it, the Hollywood tradition of Jesus begins.

2

I WAS A TEENAGE JESUS IN COLD WAR AMERICA: *KING OF KINGS*, 1961

REMAKING THE AMERICAN CHRIST

So powerful an icon was DeMille's *King of Kings* that Hollywood did not attempt a new presentation of its Cinematic Savior in a Jesus film until 1961, despite the fact that through the 1950s religiously themed spectaculars dominate a significant portion of Hollywood productions and profits. Films like *Quo Vadis, Ben-Hur,* and DeMille's final and perhaps best epic, *The Ten Commandments,* continued to put on the screen for American audiences a heightened view of themselves as a true Christian nation. Despite its appearance and the indications of its title, Nicholas Ray's *King of Kings* of 1961 was not simply a remake of the 1927 *King of Kings,* but rather was the first attempt by Hollywood to tell the entire life story of Jesus from birth to death. The film establishes Jesus as the Messiah of Peace, with his mythic polar opposite, Jesus Barabbas, as the Messiah of War. Jesus Christ, played by a young Jeffrey Hunter, becomes the representative of a new type of American man whose entire look and action contrasts starkly with the old American man of action, Barabbas, played by Rod Taylor. By transforming the largely external ethical drama of good versus evil into an internalized dynamic directed at producing a truly new spiritual man, the film fails to tap into the deeper resources of spectacle, action, and divine mystery that made *King of Kings* (1927) so successful. It nevertheless gives us an opportunity to understand the new directions prescribed for the American Christ at the height of the Cold War and on the eve of the dramatic alterations to American consciousness of the 1960s.

Significantly more than in the earlier *King of Kings* (1927), the *King of Kings* of 1961 shows the marks of increasing independence of the filmic Christ from church control, which permits a weakening of epic and communal values in favor of a new exploration of Christ as an individual, an exploration of the so-called secular influences of the American "doctrine" of individualism.

Unfortunately, while it has points of interest cinematically, as art, even popular art, this film is a cinematic failure. First and foremost this is because the performances, including those by Jeffrey Hunter and Rod Taylor, simply are not up to the dramatic tasks set by the script, which makes them stark mythic polarities. The exception may be the portrayal of Judas by Rip Torn. At deeper levels, moreover, the film fails because it requires a conception of Jesus as an introspective American hero trying to find himself. This runs headlong into the cultural restrictions still in place. The American Christ, and with him America, cannot yet face his own doubts about his humanity and still fulfill his divine role.

The biblical spectacular was, as we have seen, virtually invented by DeMille and required sex, sadism, and melodrama. Ultimately melodrama when combined with biblical material becomes a morality play. The theology of the film loses much of its direct reference to God and concentrates on the human. *King of Kings* (1961) attempts to resolve the problems of both public and private ethics within the inner man. Thus, the problems of politics are subsumed under the rubric of the "New Man," and Jesus as Messiah of Peace remains predominantly human. He points the way forward toward the perfectibility of each individual American as the New Man. The issue of God lurks in the background, sanctifying the search, but never directly addressed. The film also provides an alternative, or foil, to Jesus in Jesus Barabbas, Messiah of War. According to the iconography of the film he is to be seen as the Old Man of the violent American past. The film unintentionally reveals a destabilization of the main character Jesus, because Barabbas, as a man of action, fits more perfectly the ideal of American film's heroic tradition evoked by the very genre, the biblical spectacular, in which the film is shot. Our expectations of the genre are disappointed by the behavior of this new Jesus, and so we have difficulty accepting him.

JESUS, JESUS BARABBAS, AND JUDAS: A NEW TRIANGLE

Little exception can be taken to the film's representation of Jesus as a child, but from the moment the adult Jesus appears at his baptism by John, there are substantial digressions from older representations. He is young, blond, and blue-eyed. Nor does God call from the heavens at his baptism. Thus, the event is preserved on a low-key and mundane plane and no direct symbols of divine presence occur.

As he subsequently wanders in the desert, the film depicts Jesus' temptations as almost exclusively inner, indicated by auditory and visionary experiences shot from Jesus' perspective. No bread appears on screen, nor does Satan take him to the pinnacle of the temple of Jerusalem as in Matthew or Luke. We see from Jesus' perspective the temptation to world power as an oriental, "Arabian nights" cityscape. Jesus' own religious experience remains internal throughout the film. If there is a theological center to the film, then it resides in Jesus as the iconic Messiah of Peace who opposes and is opposed by sadism, totalitarianism, and violence. Nevertheless, the audience receives no clue as to his internal struggle or divine inspiration to arrive at this spiritual plateau. The film seems to presume divine presence while at the same time denying us a clear view of either the descent of God to Jesus or conversely of Jesus' ascent to divine awareness. As in *King of Kings* (1927), the film constructs a melodramatic triangle. This time, however, the film does not foreground the conversion of female sexuality, but rather Jesus converts the inner person as subsequent events make clear. The triangle of conversion is Jesus–Barabbas–Judas.

The film dedicates much time and effort to establishing the necessity and legitimacy of envisioning and accepting Jesus as the Messiah of Peace. Despite painstaking technological strategies to highlight the message of the film, the portrayal of Jesus is not powerful enough to carry the audience along with that message. In an attempt to establish Jesus as the Messiah of Peace, the Sermon on the Mount provides the crucial theological scene for the film. In it, Jesus makes his case for the transformation of the inner man to the way of peace. All of the major characters who have a potential for conversion have gathered to hear Jesus: Lucius, Claudia, Barabbas, Judas. Directorially, the scene represents a tour de force. The shot involved a track for a dolly of 160 feet on a 58-degree slope that took more than a month to prepare. Within the scene there were more than 81 setups, and it took 21 days to shoot.[1]

Whereas DeMille, using silent film, emphasized an action-oriented Jesus, Ray, with sound, could dedicate almost 15 minutes to providing viewers with an idealized compendium of Jesus' teachings. During the scene Jesus is virtually the only speaker. Even a great large-screen actor has difficulty holding audience attention for such a monologue; unfortunately Jeffrey Hunter is not well suited to the requirements. In style and structure the scene epitomizes the conventions of mainstream American Protestant worship. The pace of delivery is slow and measured. The camera tends to go for medium and long shots, seldom using close-ups that might have provided a sense of intimacy. But that also might tend to suggest the divine sense of Christ.

The scene achieves some intimacy by showing Jesus engaging with specific individuals or groups as he walks up the mountain. No variation of pitch or pace portrays emotion. Long takes provide a stage for Jesus to deliver his sermon. If Jesus is to be seen as other, then his otherness is one of emotional detachment. Emotional quietism characterizes his piety and the piety of his audience. Indeed, sparseness of emotion and drama when Jesus is on screen characterizes the film. His sermon ends with a concluding benediction and musical doxology.

Jesus represents a secularized generic piety most akin to mainstream Protestantism. The shift from *King of Kings* (1927) here and throughout is most notable in the music, which, except for rare instances, does not reference church music. No evangelical fervor, no camp-meeting emotion, no angst marks Jesus' portrayal. Nor can we identify specific elements of ethnic, Catholic piety. Thomas Jefferson and other deists among the nation's founders would understand this movie's spiritual ambiance. We are near the apex and end of mainstream Protestant modernity in America and Hollywood film.

Jesus' mission to free the inner man comes into sharpest focus approximately one hour into the film, when Jesus visits John the Baptist in prison. Jesus speaks to Lucius, the Roman officer, "I come to free John. . . . I come to free him within his cell." Though he can come and go as he pleases, Lucius can be seen as a prisoner of the sword, constrained by his rank and his duty to imperial power, but John, the prisoner, can become free in himself through Jesus' consciousness-raising teaching.

In the scene immediately preceding this one, Judas, as interpreted by the narrator, must decide between the Messiah of Peace and the Messiah of War (Barabbas). The Messiah of Peace brings freedom to the inner man, leading him to depend on peace, not war. But as portrayed in the film, the counterpoint to Jesus is Jesus Barabbas, the Messiah of War. Rather than a simple evil opposite to Jesus' goodness, Barabbas is a man of action. The choice between them in a cinematic frame is neither so automatic nor so easy as might be assumed.

The major action sequences in the film occur in two battle scenes in which Barabbas functions as leader and would-be military savior of his people. Shot to the same effect and in virtually the same style as the typical Indian raid on the cavalry in American Westerns, which Ray had significant experience in directing, Barabbas's attack on Pilate's processional column arriving in Jerusalem provides an early introduction to Barabbas, the Old Man and freedom fighter. The scene is crosscut with the preaching of John the Baptist and the baptism of Jesus. Barabbas and Lucius fight *mano-a-mano* at the conclusion of the scene. Barabbas escapes to fight another day. The melodrama is established. The expectations for the American action hero derived from Westerns establish the vivid dramatic frisson for the remainder of the movie. Hunter's Jesus is not capable of inspiring a corresponding expectation.

The second major battle scene substitutes for the cleansing of the temple in canonical sources. Jesus makes a triumphal entry into the temple amid hosannas. (Note that the scene directly reuses the camera work of *King of Kings* [1927].) Once Jesus is inside the temple, Barabbas starts his revolt. The inexorable imperial might of Rome, embodied by its army, literally marches over and crushes the insurrectionists. Barabbas, imprisoned, remains the dramatic foil to Jesus.

Dramatic structure provides a key to understanding the mythic structure of the film. Jesus of Nazareth is the mythic opposite to Jesus Barabbas. The Messiah of Peace opposes the Messiah of War. Whereas the concepts of War and Peace can be grasped, the film, by personifying these opposites as active characters, encourages the viewer to seek resolutions or balances through the vicarious overcoming of obstacles in the person of the character. Because of the presumptions that the viewer brings to this movie, the initial response that the movie evokes and presumes is one of siding with Jesus. But in this film the opposites of peace and war are associated with alternative depictions of manhood. This polarized structure of opposites—Old Man, New Man—provides no middle-ground for the viewer or other characters in the film. All must choose.

Judas, the third member of the dramatic triangle, occupies a relatively equal place of dramatic interest. He does not offer any escape from the polarization of Judas and Barabbas, since he too must choose between the two. Unlike *King of Kings* (1927), neither greed nor the desire for political power motivates Judas. He originally follows Barabbas in the quest for freedom by means of violent action. He starts in the camp of the Old Man, but ends betraying the New. This idea of Judas as freedom fighter is based upon the suggestion by some scholars that Judas's second name *Iscariot* refers to the Latin *sicarus*, referring to a dagger easily hidden in one's clothes and thus a favorite weapon of assassins. Unfortunately for the theory, nowhere do the Gospels suggest that Judas was motivated by anything other than money, or Satan.

In the development of the movie, the crucial scene for Judas is when en route with Barabbas to see Jesus he witnesses the saving of Magdalene from stoning. The option stated for Judas by the omniscient narrator (perhaps a stand-in for God, voiced by Orson Welles, who dissociated himself from the movie and refused to be credited) is also the option for the viewer. Will he follow the Messiah of War or the Messiah of Peace? The film presumes that the viewer is familiar with the biblical story sufficiently to know that Judas will betray. We do not wish to be Judases.

As the inevitable tragic subplot unfolds, however, Judas fails to make a clear choice. Salvation in American religious thought must be achieved through conversion, through an act of willful decision. Convicted of one's sinful pathway, the individual sinner makes a new choice for Jesus. Judas makes the fatal mistake of trying to bring the two Messiahs together; he tries to hold the mythic dyad of war and peace together. So he plots with the leaderless Zealots after the capture of Barabbas, "I will force his hand. Once he feels the Roman sword at his throat he will strike them down with the wave of one arm." On the surface of the story, Judas has clearly misunderstood the power of Jesus, which derives from peace. On the level of myth structure, he attempts to treat mythic polarities as if they can be resolved into each other. In the terms of the myth of the film, you cannot make war to find peace. In juxtaposing the thesis (Jesus) with the antithesis (Barabbas) he hopes to arrive at a negotiated settlement (synthesis) between both strategies. Jesus will become, according to Judas's thinking, both the Prince of Peace and the apocalyptic Son of Man who comes with his angels to judge.

Such a solution has its roots in canonical Christian thought. Matthew, Mark, and Luke each in its own way preserves an anticipation of the return of Jesus as militant, judge, and Son of Man at the end of time. Most vividly, Revelation (John's Apocalypse) depicts the final battle of Christ and his angelic minions against Satan and his followers. This apocalyptic theology preserves for subsequent Christian cultures a vision of the final righteous judgment of God.

In *King of Kings* (1961), however, Judas does not adopt the biblical perspective that counsels passive waiting for the return of Christ to judge. His misunderstanding of Jesus in the film and perhaps poor timing in relationship to the biblical tradition is his fatal flaw. The narrator emphasizes Judas's mistake as he goes into Caiaphas's house to betray Jesus, "to test and prove forever the divine power of the Messiah." To test the Messiah, the narrator suggests, is a fatal error. In Judas's view Jesus and Barabbas are "left and right hands of the same body." No trial before the Sanhedrin and no betrayal occur in the film.

THE SIGNIFICANCE OF ROMAN IMPERIAL OPPRESSION

The triangle of drama constructed by Jesus–Barabbas–Judas plays against the political backdrop of Roman oppression. The opening six minutes of film, constructed as historical context for the life of Jesus, provide a view of the fundamental character of Roman power. Pompey invades and conquers Jerusalem, slaughtering the high priest by his own hand. He finds in the Holy of Holies of the temple only the law of Moses. Jews are slaughtered, burned, made slaves. The analogy to the Nazi Holocaust is transparent. In relationship to the use of the Herodians in the film, discussed below, it also becomes apparent that Rome suggests Soviet totalitarianism—in the early 1960s Egypt and Syria were regarded as client states of the Soviet Union.

Three characters define Roman presence for the film's audience and invite its associations: Pontius Pilate, his wife Claudia, and Lucius, his commander. Pilate remains in imperial opposition to Jesus throughout the film. A drive for political power characterizes him. Throughout the trial he never waivers from the position of Roman imperial power, totalitarian authority. The charge reported by Caiaphas from Judas that Jesus is a political threat is sufficient for Pilate to judge him.

Pilate alone accepts responsibility for the judgment of Jesus. He represents atheistic, secular power. Surprisingly, for those who know Roman history, this movie, like many others of the 1950s, shows Romans as neither religious nor pious. It is as if they really don't believe in their gods or rituals. Rather they are an atheistic, secular state. The discussion with Jesus about the "Truth" in the trial scene, therefore, holds little theological meaning for Pilate.

The film adopts a further conceit probably in reference to American history that depicts Romans, and here Pilate, with an English accent. Hence, our own story of the English oppression that brings on the American Revolution becomes coded in Hollywood as representing any "once upon a time" oppression. There may be a suggestion of effete sadism on Pilate's part as well; he decides to have Jesus scourged because, "He is different." Pilate wants to break Jesus.

If Pilate maintains a Roman film presence as representative of atheistic totalitarian power, its potential conversion is developed by analogy with the characters of Claudia and Lucius. From her hearing of John the Baptist onward, the film shows Claudia as a potential convert. She hears with keen interest Lucius's reports on Jesus' activities. Eventually she goes with Lucius to the Sermon, where she appears nearly convinced of Jesus' message.

The ubiquitous Lucius is a fictionalized tie to all elements of the film. He is the good soldier. He refuses initially to participate in the slaughter of the innocent children in Bethlehem by Herod the Great. He overlooks the nonenrollment of the 12-year-old Jesus. He provides access for Jesus to John the Baptist in prison. Most importantly he is the honorable opponent of Barabbas. He frees Barabbas, saying, "Look on him who is dying for you," thereby evangelizing Barabbas and, through him, the audience.

THE ARABS

The lurid sadomasochistic and sexual interest in the film comes in the persons of Herod Antipas, Herodias, and Salome. Herod and his court occur in 70mm Technicolor splendor. Herodias and Salome provide caricatures of female sadomasochism and vanity. Herod himself lusts palpably for Salome, promising her even her mother's throne. Her sexualized dance, her navel covered by a small upright snake, suggests she has even stolen her stepfather's phallic power. In the portrayal of Salome, Herod, and Herodias, the film draws on long tradition in the Christian West that culminated in a play by Oscar Wilde, visual art by Aubrey Beardsley, and an opera by Richard Strauss.[2]

Most surprisingly from an historical perspective is the Herodians' identification as "Arab." Josephus, the first-century Jewish historian, suggests in one passage that Herod the Great was from an Idumean woman, thus not really Jewish, but ethnic Palestinian. The development in this film, however, that assigns to the Herodians the most brutal and savage suppression of the Jews under the title of Arab is a clear indication of the politics of the film in 1961. Therefore, Babbington and Evans rightly suggest that the Herodians are used as analogues to the contemporary threat of the Arab world against Israel.[3] The film falls into a rather nonreflective orientalism. *King of Kings* (1961) uses the Romans as analogue to Soviet totalitarianism and in the deep background of course is reference to Hitler's and Stalin's atrocities against the Jews. The anxieties of Cold War international politics are projected back onto the mythological time of Jesus. His confrontations are ours.

ETHIC IDENTIFIERS IN *KING OF KINGS* (1961)

The historical conceit of the film is that Jesus, Barabbas, the disciples—in short all of the people on the screen except the Romans and Arabs—are Jewish. The visual depiction, however, leaves little doubt that the downtrodden Jews are in reality white Americans, albeit with bad beards. The movie visually strips the story of Jesus of any grounding in first-century Judaism, its culture, its institutions. Instead, the film constructs a Technicolor playground for American self-exploration.

Only two blacks appear. The first is one of the magi who appear at the birth of Jesus (Balthazar, perhaps). The second scourges Jesus. The contrast in the scourging scene is made the more striking since Jesus is so very white and his paleness is enhanced by the choice to remove all of his visible body hair, including from his armpits. The alabaster New Man is beaten by the black African. The scene, both sadistic and homoerotic, is suffused with a white fear of black uprising, and considering that the movie was released in 1961 in the midst of the Civil Rights movement, we are justified in asking whether the movie participates in a cultural inscription of white fear of black reprisal.

The film continues the tendency begun by DeMille to de-emphasize possible Jewish responsibility for the death of Jesus. The film also draws on the energy of post-WWII biblical scholarship as well as initial American insensitivity to the Nazi Holocaust (both unavailable to DeMille) to eliminate Jewish culpability for the death of Jesus. To this end, Caiaphas and official Judaism play virtually no role in the life and death of Jesus.

The elimination of an obvious Jewish presence in *King of Kings* (1961) can be interpreted both positively and negatively. It takes into account a long history of anti-Semitism in the Christian West that held the Jews as a people eternally responsible for the death of the Christ. *Justice at Nuremberg*, also released in 1961, will win two Academy Awards for depicting Nazi guilt for Holocaust atrocities.

Historical biblical scholarship, which also participates in the history and culture of America, increasingly postulates after WWII that the Gospels embody anti-Judaism. The earliest Christians were Jewish. According to this emerging consensus of scholarship, the Gospel writers would have obvious reasons for playing down the culpability of the Romans for the death of Jesus. It was dangerous for these early Christians to claim Rome as crucifier of their Lord. As Christians of the second and third generations became more dominantly non-Jewish, the natural tendency was to blame Jesus' death on the Jewish authorities. In real historical terms, it is unlikely that Pilate or any Roman official would have signed off on the Crucifixion and "washed his hands" of the whole affair.

King of Kings (1961) adapts this relatively new, at the time, historical finding in service to its depiction of Rome as the totalitarian atheistic state. Rome is not America in this movie; therefore, it can play the role of evil empire.

More subtly, the elimination of Jewish culture as the context for Jesus' life and ministry confirms an anti-Jewish tendency in American culture and film. If a film represents Jesus as us, then we assume him to be a nice white American boy. There is nothing foreign or other about this Jesus.

Indeed only the Romans, who are typed as foreign by their accents, or the Herodians, who are oriental in style, appear as anything other than normal, clean Americans, albeit in "biblical" dress. The casting and typing mean a seamless bridge to a golden mythical age where contemporary Americans can safely resolve their problems of identity and destiny in the company of their Jesus. Like the overt anti-Arabism, the covert erasure of Jesus' Jewishness bespeaks an underlying cinematic and cultural anti-Semitism. The Jewish and Arabic problems are two sides of the same hand. One is the alien other in our midst, the other the alien other who threatens us from outside. Whereas the Arabs appear as other, the Jews are rejected as a cultural entity and basically erased.

The Christ is not Jewish. He is the New Man, who is America.

THE WOMEN OF JESUS' HOUSE

King of Kings (1961) continues the film tradition of enhancing the role of Mary the Mother. Mary knows Jesus' mission perhaps better than does Jesus himself. In the home scene just prior to Jesus' entry into Jerusalem he is interrupted while mending a chair. Showing Jesus in private scenes as a carpenter becomes a staple of the Hollywood Christ tradition—it will recur to humorous effect as recently as *The Passion of the Christ*. He promises that he will finish the job when he returns. But she knows he will never return.

Mary forms with Magdalene and the disciple John a new holy household, or family. By implication this is the nucleus of the new household, and may also be seen as alluding to the church, especially as depicted in the Gospel of John. The mother is played by an Irish actress, Siobhan McKenna. She retains her brogue throughout. In the modern film culture of America, one of the quintessential types is the Irish mother. Here Hollywood provides one for Jesus. The film indicates thereby a tip of the hat to American Catholics. It also represents in its casting and characterization a nostalgia for the simple agrarian, working-class piety for which the Irish mother is a ready symbol, reminding us of an America that no longer exists by 1961.

I would note that the Jesus as working carpenter image is well illustrated by the Bruce Barton bestseller *The Man Nobody Knows*. As noted in the previous chapter, he served as advisor on the first *King of Kings*. In that case his vision of a robust Jesus, leader of men, remained unfulfilled. The young Jesus of *King of Kings* (1961) moves in that direction, but American theology seems to be captured by an association of effetism with divine calling in this movie.

Mary's treatment, like that of Jesus, stops short of assigning any direct divine knowledge. The film indicates no miraculous conception of Jesus. Mary has no direct visitations from God.

Magdalene in *King of Kings* (1961) plays a vastly subsidiary role as compared with her role in the first *King of Kings*. She is simply the woman caught in adultery; she is in no way the representative of the courtesan female or even street prostitute. Jesus saves her from stoning and for God in the same act. She adopts the position of daughter to Mary, veiling herself in the Hollywood convention of ordered sisters. Her sexuality muted, she remains stereotyped. Since she is played by a Spanish actress, she falls into the category of dark women in the film (Claudia, Herodias, Salome). Darkness, in this case being brunette and foreign, indicates sexual sin, with its debauched and violent overtones. Two of these women, Claudia and Magdalene, ultimately choose salvation. The other two, Herodias and Salome, do not. Fallen women can receive sanctification by Jesus' forgiveness, but, apparently, not if they are Arab. Women, as in the first *King of Kings*, are used to represent private sins. Men, public.

THE CRUCIFIXION AS DRAMATIC CLIMAX

As in the Gospels, so in the movies, the Crucifixion constitutes the climax of Jesus' mission and the tragic end of his life. All of the plot threads are brought together in the final scenes of the movie. Consistent with the demythologizing style of the movie, the Crucifixion shows no signs of divine intervention. No one is judged by earthquake. Instead the viewer decides for or against Jesus without any representation of God's own perspective. Viewers are left to decide for or against Jesus based on the evidence from a human perspective.

Pilate condemns Jesus. Lucius directs Barabbas to "Look on him who is dying for you." The implication, even if muted, remains clear: The Messiah of Peace dies to save the Messiah of War. He has been privately scourged in an atmosphere for the audience of almost reverent contemplation.

The way of the cross draws heavily on images and shots already developed in *King of Kings* (1927). Jesus has a full cross; the thieves only cross bars. He bears the weight of sin. The camera provides us with a close-up of the end of his cross bumping up the road. As in previous scenes the atmosphere of quiet contemplation is preserved. The crowds do not jeer; the soldiers do not mock. Crucifixion is as solemn as a church service.

Jesus arrives on Calvary with everyone else: Barabbas, Judas, Lucius, Claudia, Mary the Mother, Magdalene, and John. The shot of the placing of the cross in the ground is the most unnerving and innovative in the scene. The perspective is from the top of the cross as it swings around and up and then jars into the ground. The resulting high shot establishes the cross as a connecting link between heaven and earth around which resolutions of the film's myth will take place. As mediator, Jesus hangs between the twin poles of the divine and human, between the camera's heavenly perspective and the earth below. The perspective, so clearly constructed by the placement of a camera on the top of the cross, however, remains equivocal. It is a human perspective, not God's. To portray God's perspective we would anticipate a high shot independent of the movement of the cross. The shot more closely accords with Jesus' own perspective. Thus we are left wondering whether there is a God in the heavens. Throughout the scene the camera will alternate from high to low providing Jesus' perspective on the characters as they contemplate the Crucifixion and decide for or against Jesus.

Judas leaves to hang himself; thereby, this film as in *King of Kings* (1927) more closely associates Judas's and Jesus' death than does the Gospel of Matthew. Barabbas later finds Judas dangling from the strap of his coin bag. The symbol remains hollow, however, since the film never constructs Judas as motivated by money. Rather, Jesus' death is inevitable, and correspondingly Judas's betrayal is a tragic, almost foreordained necessity. Judas, unable to decide between Messiahs, falls into despair and takes his own life.

HOLLYWOOD'S MAKING OF THE AMERICAN CHRIST AS NEW MAN

King of Kings (1961) attempts a full-frontal demythologizing of the Jesus story while at the same time constructing Jesus as the New Man, the America of the future. We cannot attribute this emphasis exclusively to Nicholas Ray, the director. He did not have control of the final cut.[4] Rather, the film, like most mainstream Hollywood movies, expresses a complex variety of creative visions in the dynamic spheres of American popular culture. It is a studio movie.

The producer, Samuel Bronston, also produced *El Cid* the same year. It was a major epic success starring Charlton Heston as the title character, a Christian freedom fighter against the Moors of Spain (Arabs were everywhere in 1961). Ray had experienced surprising success as the director of *Rebel Without a Cause* (1955), which became a cult classic after the tragic death of James Dean, its lead character. His previous experience was primarily in the action genres of Westerns and war movies. Philip Yordan, credited with the script, also did *El Cid*; Ray Bradbury also worked on the script but was uncredited; and Miklos Rozsa (who had also done *Ben-Hur* [1959]) provided the music. All of this is to say that the adaptation of the Jesus story in *King of Kings* (1961) is by a crew, and cast as well, whose professional and creative experience in Hollywood was primarily rooted in hero tales in the epic mode of the 1950s.

The film cost $8 million and was released with a 32-page coffee-table book. Bronston visited Pope John XXIII and received his approval.[5] Later producers (for example, Mel Gibson) will pay homage to this publicity and marketing strategy. Martin Scorsese will also express strong appreciation for Ray's camera work, especially in the Sermon on the Mount and Crucifixion scenes. He will use Ray's tracking shots and adapt them to his own intimate interpretation of Jesus in *The Last Temptation of Christ* (1988). Gibson will mimic the shot from the top of the cross in *The Passion of the Christ*.

Other filmic innovations prove less influential. The Last Supper, one of the most established scenes in popular imagination through church art, will always be compared by an American audience to da Vinci's classic painting. Here, Ray chooses to construct a Y-shaped table. He evokes thereby a reference to the impending Crucifixion. The shot, however, which could be used as a major bridge between the contemporary audience and the time of Jesus, is neither an eruption of authenticity (Jesus and the disciples probably did not sit at a picnic bench) nor does it evoke the piety of the audience.

The movie secularizes and modernizes the Christ by the removal of almost all indications of transcendence within the film. Jesus has no direct religious experience. Salvation comes about by quiet rational contemplation of the moral acts of a man in history. In service to this, the palette of 70mm Technicolor denotes the real historical plane of existence. To a twenty-first-century audience, now accustomed to the development of realistic film style and computer-generated images, the look is too storybook, but to a 1950–60s audience the new, sharper technology must have presented Jesus in a modern context, with up-to-date effects. History is sharpened, demythified.

The scenes adapted directly from the Gospels are shot sparsely. They are arranged as a worship service. The pace is slow, contemplative. Jesus, the New Man, acts within a limited range of emotion. His piercing blue eyes communicate divine otherness. His look is that of the "troubled youth" established by James Dean, spinning off of Marlon Brando. Unlike Brando or Dean, however, Jeffrey Hunter remains undeveloped. Where they revel in an exposure of raw masculine emotion, his manhood is almost extinguished. So he is neither the older, more mature

Jesus of popular imagination nor a new Jesus of compelling dynamism. The natural reaction of the audience is to see him as "not Jesus" and then to be unable to identify an aspect that might make his New Man status appealing. Ultimately, Barabbas, the quintessential Old Man of American Westerns and epics, holds more screen energy. When Hollywood shifts to a young Jesus in *Jesus Christ Superstar* and *The Last Temptation of Christ* it will allow a direct confrontation with Jesus the revolutionary and troubled New Man. Jesus will be allowed to divide the audience by his direct humanity replete with doubts.

It may be that the film was simply presenting a demythologized version of Jesus to avoid any clear denominational markers of belief that would limit the audience appeal. Jesus is reduced to straightforward human virtues. This cultural explanation coincides with the choice of Cold War religious spectacular as the genre. It expresses the major concern of power in an international community, its moral uses, the righteous citizen, the righteous nation. In religious spectacular, followers of Jesus (the church) appear as an embattled community.[6] In *King of Kings* (1961) the church, usually represented by the disciples, becomes completely identified with an America that is the pluralistic Christian mainstream. This shift already signaled by *King of Kings* (1927) means that the Christ has become a clear signifier in American movie tradition. No longer is the Christ under the control of the church. Now, Christ and the disciples, analogues for America, take on totalitarian dictatorships and their proxies.

These analogues to history and the culture of 1961 America do not, however, exhaust the meaning of this production of the American Christ. We have moved, with *King of Kings* (1961) to a juncture in America where the process of modernity demands a close examination of Jesus as the perfected man. The movie implies perfectibility for all by individual moral choices, although it stops short of showing Jesus himself making such choices. Instead subsidiary characters make their decision only in contemplation of his human life. Jesus no longer is clearly the light itself; he is the New Man that America as a collective must become by personal decision. Jesus' life reveals the next evolutionary jump for America. This jump is thoroughly male; women only tag along as acolytes. They fulfill their salvation by bearing witness to the New Man. By comparison with *King of Kings* 1927, they are noticeably less central to the story of salvation.

The movie unintentionally highlights the American dilemma: Alienated from itself, America worships Jesus and prefers Barabbas. Jesus denuded of his body hair is conversely compared with the American hero. Jesus as Son of Man fits uneasily the role of idealized heroic traditions of Hollywood masculinity. Through the 1950s that tradition undergoes significant and monumental change. Most noteworthy Marlon Brando in *A Streetcar Named Desire* and James Dean in *Rebel Without a Cause* develop a new highly sexualized anti-hero. In Dean's case, his on and off-screen persona was sexually ambivalent. He seduces both Natalie Wood and Sal Mineo on the set of *Rebel*.[7] *King of Kings* (1961) might have drawn on that tradition; instead no one is ready to explore a sexualized and troubled Christ.

By appealing to the epic biblical style rather than a smaller realistic dramatic style, *King of Kings* (1961) almost guarantees the failure of its Christ. It evokes the Hollywood mainstream development of the American hero. In this mythology the hero becomes a man of violence from the necessity of liberating himself from threat or suppression of his personal liberty. Thus, even Moses (Charlton Heston) in *The Ten Commandments* can be the direct heroic agent of a vengeful and righteous God as he lifts his staff to call down the waters over the armies of Pharaoh. Or Judah Ben-Hur (Charlton Heston again) can be transformed in the last reel after much violent struggle by the unseen Christ. America needs the catharsis of righteous vengeance for wrongs done to our heroes. We prefer for this vengeance to occur on screen. The canonical story of Jesus, which at best postpones the visitation of God's vengeance against Jesus' enemies until some future date of Jesus' return, provides little heroic catharsis. Jesus fits poorly into the heroic model. In American movie tradition, he is an unsatisfying Messiah of Peace unless he first picks up a gun.

The Jesus of *King of Kings* (1961) shows us an America unsure of its future or present. He really denotes the deeper anxiety; if America is so virtuous, so nice, why do so many oppose us? The problem is American self-perception. If Jesus is America, the moral good guy, and America is opposed, American perception is wrong. The film's answer to the problems of domestic and foreign policy demands an inward turn of the individual. But others do not cooperate.

King of Kings (1961) and America fail to capture the Gospels' subtle understanding of evil as both interior and exterior power. They reject Jesus' revolutionary action in associating, indeed elevating, sinners, women, and the poor against polite, middle-class churchgoers or their analogues in his day. Hence, Jesus has no real conflict in the movie that explains his death, because in this Hollywood American Christ, Jesus does not offend the establishment, which is us. As long as Jesus is a symbol of personal integration and salvation, America will absorb him into its story of itself as good guy. Opposition is always by the recalcitrant, irrational outsider. We are the good Christ, no threat to anyone unless they are insanely evil.

3

THE GREATEST STORY EVER TOLD:
SUBURBAN JESUS AND THE
MORTGAGED GOSPEL

THE FINAL PROTESTANT EPIC

Nicholas Ray in making *King of Kings* (1961) may have assumed the title of Demille's classic *King of Kings* (1927), but he failed dramatically. The main cause of this failure was an inability to make his view of Jesus fit into the model of American epic hero. Thereby, the film, while it advocated the conversion of inner man to a true ethical spirituality, was frustrated in its attempt to convince. George Stevens, in *The Greatest Story Ever Told* (1965), takes up the challenge of the epic genre for a final time. He continues the movement away from the supernatural conflict of good and evil and toward the ethical, as did Ray, while at the same time seeking to reincorporate the more traditional view of theology found in DeMille's film. In *The Greatest Story Ever Told* Stevens presumes that the Protestant mainstream audience that was his throughout the bulk of his career, especially in 1950s Hollywood, continues into the mid-60s.

As the analysis of *The Greatest Story Ever Told* will show, he was mistaken. The title of the film itself indicates a mistaken attempt at merchandising, the product having been diluted in the interest of universalizing and the target audience perceived through the fogged window of nostalgia. The engagement with the myth of the Christ and the attempt to project that myth as a timeless American persona drive the film. The film faces the problem, however, that the unified, mainstream Protestant consensus about who we are as America no longer commands assent from the audience, and the film shows the cracks. Standing as direct evidence for mainline Protestantism's loss of the power to define and unify America, it simultaneously also represents the last gasp of the big studio system, and with it, the epic spectacular style.

The Greatest Story Ever Told does accept the myth of the Christ as authentic and theologically pivotal, though it may in fact take too much for granted in doing so. Its Christ descends from the heavens to offer salvation to humanity before re-ascending to the heavens. Throughout, the Christ knows, and the audience knows, that he is God. Consequently, the dramatic tension of the Gospels' stories, taken collectively, is negated. The manifest triumph and divinity of Christ is further represented on screen by the use of a Byzantine-style church dome at the beginning and end of the film. In both shots the actor who plays Jesus, Max von Sydow, is depicted as Jesus as part of the mural on the dome.

This visual icon of the film indicates its overriding theology. Like the Gospel of John, to which it constantly refers, *The Greatest Story Ever Told* implies a clear dualism of above/below. The heavenly realm, the realm of God and the Word, descends into an earthly incarnation in the person of Jesus. Salvation then becomes an inward journey of the human to unity with the heavenly realm. Jesus is not of this world. He saves us out of the world into a universal and spiritual perfection.

While the film reproduces in large measure the viewpoint of the Gospel of John, it cannot reproduce (and significantly makes little attempt to do so) its social and historical location or impact. The Johannine tradition, by contrast with the Americanized geographic and ethnic landscape of the film, took shape within a thoroughly Jewish culture. The author and original audience lived within a sectarian Jewish group who believed that Jesus was the Christ, the Logos of God. They narrate their understanding of themselves as "born from above" (John 3:3). Their world is separate from the material World of Evil.

The director, cast, crew, and audience of *The Greatest Story Ever Told* conceive of themselves as part of a good, savable, and Christian world in trouble. The film attempts to reconfigure mainstream cultural myth by adapting ancient mythic structures. The resulting art loses drama, the frisson that comes from a depth perception of dualistic endangerment in the world. It comes to play like a Sunday school lesson, without the real danger of unfaith. *The Greatest Story Ever Told* fails dramatically because it cannot overcome the divide between the original text's ancestry and the film's own American culture. It constructs an alien Christ governed by nostalgia for preindustrial, premodern faith rather than creative engagement with current life in is own culture.

The film went through a tortured production and release. At least two and maybe three versions were released. The first Hollywood Screening came in at 225 minutes, the London release at 197. The general American release was 141 minutes. There is even some disagreement on this history: Other scholars find only two versions, one at 260 minutes and the other at 190.[1]

JESUS THE ETERNAL LOGOS INCARNATE

Jesus is the eternal Logos of God now incarnate, the Word made Flesh. The film subsumes all other characterizations to this mythological and theological claim. In keeping with this theme the film lacks what one of my students, Julia Haneke, dubbed "God shots," camera high shots, usually from directly overhead, the perspective of which can only be that of God. Such shots occur frequently in films, surprisingly there is even one in *Ghost in the Shell*, a classic Japanese anime film.

The context of a scene determines whether God's view is actually being invoked. Jesus in *The Greatest Story Ever Told* is from the first frame God on earth; God's perspective is Jesus' and can be shown horizontally. Even the use of a helicopter shot to introduce the preaching of John the Baptist remains within the realm of the human, as John's own voice narrates. The dominating movement of camera is from the lower left to the upper right of the screen.[2] The human ascends toward the divine.

The Greatest Story Ever Told also brackets two signature events. Trumpeters herald the birth of Jesus from the walls of Jerusalem. The motif repeats itself as they also announce the Resurrection. The film further divides naturally into two dramatic parts. The first part runs from the birth of Jesus to the raising of Lazarus, news of whom comes to the walls of Jerusalem just prior to intermission. The second act after intermission moves inside Jerusalem and depicts the final week of Jesus' life.

The structure follows closely the Gospel of John. It exploits the opposition between countryside and city found also in *King of Kings* (1961). Up to intermission little opposition to Jesus occurs. He teaches, gathers disciples, works some low-key miracles, and awakens the faith of the common people of the land. The dramatic raising of Lazarus jars the viewer by contrast with the previous miracles. Once inside the urban environment of Jerusalem, we encounter the opposition in the persons of Herod, Caiaphas, Sorek (his henchman), and Pilate. Faith finds Jesus in the simple countryside and life of the village. Unfaith occurs in the power and wealth of the city. Here *The Greatest Story Ever Told* expresses nostalgia for the quickly disappearing simple faith of our ancestors and locates the challenge to American faith in the power and political corruption of the city. The image of Jesus over the prosperous city of industrial America that ended *King of Kings* will not be repeated.

Within the film the landscape is utilized as a major mythic symbol, representing alternately the barrenness and promise of the American spiritual life. It constitutes the audience's bridge to the story of Jesus. The film places Jesus in the same landscape as do American Westerns, with locations such as those pioneered by John Ford. While Monument Valley does not appear, locations in Utah and Nevada (with at least one scene, the Sermon on the Mount, set on the most recognizable feature of American geography, the Grand Canyon) provide the backdrop to Jesus' wanderings and teachings.

Reportedly, George Stevens chose not to shoot in the Holy Land because he saw it as too unfertile and burned out.[3] Strangely, the landscape he chooses does not look fertile. Instead the villages of Israel appear pueblo-like, perched at the foot of massive cliffs. The faith of the people of the country is simple, receptive, ready to be awakened, like the desert in which they dwell. The movie presents a direct evocation of the American West, a West that was opened by missionaries, evangelists, and farmers who converted the land and its inhabitants to productive Christian life and values. Or so reads the familiar myth. All *The Greatest Story Ever Told* lacks is a Spanish mission church. Here the stand-in is a Jewish synagogue.

Unfortunately, *The Greatest Story Ever Told* dwarfs the intimacy of Jesus' teaching and ministry by giving it this grand setting. It lacks any detailed representation of the culture of Palestine beyond that necessary to establish simple verisimilitude. It compensates by dramatic engagements in the story of John the Baptist, Lazarus, and to some extent the Crucifixion. Overall the landscape serves to absorb Jesus into the timeless myth of America. The universal Logos now is contextualized as the America that has also been exported throughout the world by Hollywood in the form of popular Westerns.

Pier Passolini's film of the same period provides an instructive contrast to the use of landscape in *The Greatest Story Ever Told*. In *Il Vangelo Matteo (The Gospel of Matthew)*, the Italian director suggestively uses the smaller, more rugged countryside of his native Calabria. His locations set the Jesus story against medieval architecture that seems to grow naturally out of the land. This suggestive, and at times surreal, use of location lets the Italian audience know that what they are watching is being interpreted for them; authenticity or reconstruction are not primary.

The Greatest Story Ever Told, for its part, contains too many mixed messages to allow the audience an uncluttered engagement. An authentic Bible story set in a clearly recognizable American desert and featuring a Christ with a Swedish accent creates confusion. Is this film intentionally convoluted, or is the merging of the biblical and the American here simply a reflection of our culture's inability to look at the past without absorbing it into the American experience as well? In the attempt to universalize the Christ, the film founders on its American cultural specificity. Still, *The Greatest Story Ever Told* instructs us about the peculiarities and pitfalls that occur between American self-perception and projection and our dedication to something like a canonical image of Jesus.

If the film were less concerned with authenticity, then another location might have let us see the contrast between fertile agrarian life and faith and the industrialized centers of corruption and power. *The Greatest Story Ever Told* remains captured by the myth of the American West as frontier and avoids the real edge of suburban development in 1960s America. Stevens treats the needs of a pious suburbia and suburban faith by integrating the contemporary world with the mythic timelessness of the Christ. The result leaves no doubt that America's future, like its past, belongs to Christianity. The question is what kind of Christian nation will we become?

LAZARUS, JUDAS, AND THE DARK HERMIT

A comparison of Judas to Lazarus helps further resolve the film's view of belief and salvation. Jesus and his disciples renounce the world. They dress in white, abandon settled life, and become homeless, itinerant, religious philosophers. They seem to be a select band of ascetics set aside for a particular mission during the lifetime of Jesus, the awakening of Israel's wayward faith. The film shares the traditional Protestant view of a temporary asceticism for the purpose of reward in the heavens.

In this tableau Lazarus becomes an important focus. His own faith represents that of the faithful, middle-class suburbanite. He gives of his wealth to the poor. In this context, Jesus, far from opposing wealth, notes only that it can be a burden. You cannot serve two masters, but Jesus is not opposed to money. He does not recommend that you leave everything and follow him. Unlike the message embedded in other passages of the Gospels, here (as in the suburbia of the viewers), riches are not the problem, transformation of the inner man is. In truth, then, *The Greatest Story Ever Told* proclaims a theological view of wealth more closely akin to Barton's view than that we found in DeMille.

Lazarus and his sisters live in a suburb of Jerusalem in a modest house (a ranch with a porch-patio). The male is head of the household, which is maintained by the sisters. Lazarus and his family represent the current and future of American suburban faith.

And it is Lazarus who provides the opportunity for the reawakening of lost American faith. The scene of his raising at first glance appears out of keeping with the depiction of miracles elsewhere in the film. Previously, the film has avoided showing nature miracles such as Jesus' walking on water. Thereby, it reduces possible objections to the suspension of natural laws by the modern audience. In terms of drama the scene of the raising of Lazarus eclipses Jesus' own Resurrection.

The important element of the scene is not the miracle of Lazarus's return from death, but the carefully orchestrated reaction shots on the part of the people gathered outside the tomb. The scene also contributes a brilliant view of the opening of the tomb from the perspective of inside—Lazarus's view of the tomb. While the scene, like the entire movie, has the pace of a sermon, cinematically it is beautiful to watch. Jesus' gesture as he prays over the tomb, for example, evokes sorrow and hope at the same moment. The shot becomes an icon for Hollywood. Scorsese will use the same perspective from inside the tomb in his interpretation in *The Last Temptation of Christ*.

Before the arrival of Jesus the movie shows that Israel has lost its way. The Romans and most of all their puppet religious officials have beaten the faith and hope out of Israel. The Romans, Herodians, and officials of the temple continually conspire to stop both John the Baptist and Jesus. Because the raising of Lazarus occurs directly on screen, it, and not Jesus' Resurrection, becomes the miracle that evokes faith and hope for the people and for the audience.

Significantly, Judas refuses to watch the scene, but its results awaken faith as represented by three witnesses, significantly, not of the disciple band. They see, believe, and proclaim to the walls of Jerusalem that the Christ has arrived. From this scene onward, the wall divides the people of the land from the urban capital, Jerusalem. Unfaith dwells within the walls of power; true faith dwells without.

Moreover, the supplied character of the Dark Hermit (Donald Pleasence) provides the incarnation of evil to act as the antagonist to Jesus. After his baptism, Jesus climbs. His ascension up the desert mountain, an allusion to Sinai and Moses, halts for a time of temptation at the cave of the Dark Hermit. Satan appears thoroughly naturalized. By the end of the scene, however, the audience cannot doubt that this Hermit is a reference to Satan himself. He opposes and knows Jesus as Son of God. He cannot be read as the simple externalization of Jesus' human consciousness. Nor is he the disembodied voice of *King of Kings* (1961). Nor the richly dressed, handsome man of *King of Kings* (1927). He now enters Hollywood film tradition as a somewhat scruffy primitive, who advocates the easy life that leads to world power and personal invincibility.

Satan makes five more appearances in the movie. Each provides a critical turning point for the story. Satan has a continuing presence unmatched by any on-screen character except for Jesus and perhaps Judas. He becomes the motivator of evil action and the exposer of human frailty. Accordingly, he appears at the stoning of Magdalene. The scene, as in *King of Kings* (1961), splits the believers from the opposition to Jesus. Satan filters through the crowd and greets Jesus with the words, "Hail, Son of David." Jesus meets him with an icy stare then looks left off screen, whence Magdalene enters. The quotation used here by being placed in the mouth of Satan establishes that the title as a reference to the earthly throne of David is an incorrect understanding. In the Gospels the title is used variously and never in the mouth of Satan. Later, when Judas at Caesarea says that Jesus is a king, we know that he aligns himself with this wrong and evil view. Jesus is not a political threat, his kingdom is not of this world; rather, he is God's Logos, the Word.

In his remaining appearances Satan acts as motivator and tempter. As Judas goes to betray Jesus he brushes past Satan in the doorway. He passes from light to darkness. Satan exists in the shadows. Unlike the Gospels, it is Satan who accuses Peter and provokes his denial. He is present in the entourage as the crown of thorns is placed on Jesus' head. In his final appearance he urges on the chant for Jesus' Crucifixion.

Satan in this movie wields no apocalyptic supernatural power, thus his designation in the credits as the Dark Hermit. The battle with Jesus is for human souls, not the territory of creation. Satan never jeopardizes Jesus, just as Jesus never jeopardizes the kings on earth; they each occupy a distinct and separate realm, despite their conflict. His costuming here, however, will form the basis of Satan's supernatural depiction in *The Passion of the Christ*. In *The Greatest Story Ever Told* his characterization shows the modern tendency to demythologize traditional Christian views where it can.

Because Satan seems to wield no unusual powers save those of a good psychologist, the viewer has trouble accounting for the betrayal of Judas. *The Greatest Story Ever Told* elevates him to the position of the first disciple called. He appears to hang back throughout the film, never becoming as fervent as the others. In the scene of the attempted stoning of Magdalene he can be glimpsed standing on a low wall, dispassionately surveying the scene. Later he tentatively misidentifies Jesus as a king. He questions the costly anointing. But each of these scenes is so tentative that betrayal of the teacher comes almost as a surprise, except that we know that Judas must betray. "I will give him to you if you promise no harm will come to him." He is "a pure, kind, man." Judas never reaches belief, nor does he seem to have the passion needed to betray. Money does not motivate him; he refuses payment from Caiaphas. While *The Greatest Story Ever Told* shows strong interest in Judas's motivations, it supplies few conclusions.

Continuing the Hollywood tradition begun in *King of Kings* (1927), *The Greatest Story Ever Told* crosscuts the death of Judas with Jesus'. As Jesus goes up the Via Dolorosa, Judas walks through the temple court. We see Jesus led up Golgotha through a city gate. Judas walks up the stairs to the altar fire. The nail is placed against Jesus' hand (see the same shot in *The Passion of the Christ*). We hear it struck. Judas falls into the fire.

What is going on? The scene is completely unique. It has no identifiable precedent in Hollywood or Christian tradition. It is, therefore, an indication of the intent of the director, a crucial clue to the point of view of the film. Judas becomes the final sacrifice of the Jerusalem temple. At this point in the film, symbolically, God is still present. Subsequent to Judas's suicide, Jesus dies outside the wall of Jerusalem as the first and only sacrifice of the New Covenant. After Jesus' death, the temple veil appears open, with a wind blowing it outward. God has left the temple.

In this depiction of Judas's suicide, the film adopts a direct form of American Christian successionism that we have already seen in *King of Kings* (1927). Israel, conceived of as the locus of Old Testament faith, has been left behind. The symbol of Judas's suicide in the altar fire indicates that he is the last of the sacrifices in a temple that no longer worships God. He rejected Jesus, betrayed him. *The Greatest Story Ever Told* makes Judas's betrayal symbolically of a piece with Judaism's rejection of the Christ. I will develop the discussion of the pattern of successionism through the following exploration of the film's handling of the Jews and John the Baptist.

THE JEWS, ISRAEL, AND THE OLD TESTAMENT

The Greatest Story Ever Told continues the tendency in American film to reduce or eliminate responsibility for the death of Jesus from the Jews as a nation or ethnic group. At the narrative level of the film the fault lies in individual human ill will, and the film loses some of its potential melodramatic impact by distributing the responsibility among several characters: Caiaphas, Sorek, Judas, Pilate, and Herod. *King of*

Kings (1927) made the condemnation the result of Caiaphas's personal vendetta. The device of supplying the noncanonical and unique fictional role of Sorek as Caiaphas's minion, informer, and provocateur will be even more fully developed in *Jesus of Nazareth* by the role of Zerah. Hollywood tends to increase the cast list and distribute the blame. This allows for creative subplots that add dramatic action to the well-known story of Jesus. By these subplots the modern filmmakers repeatedly examine individual decision. By contrast the ancient sources show no interest in this aspect. They lack interest in personal motivation. The characters are "flat," exposed to the reader primarily through actions. The readers are then free to judge these actions for themselves in seeking the reasons and roots for the opposition to Jesus.

In the case of the Gospels generally, Caiaphas's motivation appears relatively simple: In his framework Jesus is unarguably a blasphemer. No Gospel impugns the ingenuousness of his decision; indeed in several Gospels it is made obvious in that Jesus directly claims to be the Son of God, or to have the power of God. Yes, the trial may be inappropriate, the witnesses paid off, and Caiaphas may also have political motivations, but in *The Greatest Story Ever Told* as well as in later Jesus movies, when Jesus says "I AM" or indicates that he is or has the power of God, then Caiaphas's response, while it lacks Christian faith, has good biblical support. Caiaphas is not shown in the Gospels as a conniving, atheistic unbeliever; rather he is devoted to Israel's monotheistic faith.

The Sanhedrin itself splits, with Nicodemus (Joseph Schildkraut, who played Judas in *King of Kings* [1927]) and Joseph of Arimathea leading the objections. Pilate (Telly Savalas), when presented with the case, behaves in a disinterested manner. His concern is to preserve the peace, even though his wife (Angela Lansbury) gives him some warning.

The crowds in Jerusalem are divided and stirred up by Satan. *The Greatest Story Ever Told,* using classic Christian assumptions and structure, also suggests throughout that all of this comes about according to divine plan. Jesus, with God, knows that he has come to die. All others appear to align themselves with this underlying divine will based on their faith or unfaith. The use of prophecy in the film suggests this element of divine inevitability to the audience.

Interpretation of scriptural prophecies forms a driving motivation for the actions of the Herods. The subplot also indicates for the viewer the place of modern Jews vis-à-vis America. Herod the Great (Claude Rains) knows better than his own scribes the prophecies of scripture. He believes that he can beat God and frustrate the prophecies by his own action of killing the children of Bethlehem. For him theology is a rather wooden game of power.

Likewise his son, Herod Antipas (Jose Ferrer) continues the war against fulfillment of the prophecies in his own time, turning his attention first to John the Baptist and then to Jesus. His opposition to and eventual beheading of John provides one of the strongest dramatic strains in the movie. Herod's final discussion with John is one of the finest theological discussions about the Kingdom of God on film. Herod understands the Messiah to come with earthly power that would challenge his own. John agrees with him. He understands the Christ as the bringer of judgment against evildoers, such as Herod, who need repentance. They disagree as to the Messiah's divine inevitability. Faith accepts the divine decree; unfaith tries to beat it.

In *The Greatest Story Ever Told,* there are also other developments of the Hollywood treatment of the confrontation between Herod and John. John reveals Jesus directly to Herod in a line later taken up and made famous by *The Matrix:* "He is the one." The line will be re-used in a different context in *The Last Temptation of Christ.* Moreover, Salome's dance is shrouded in darkness. Unlike *King of Kings* (1961) the film understates the sexual attraction between Herod and Salome. Her dance is exclusively for him, not in the party with his guests. The assumption seems to be that the audience knows well the story and can supply the motivation and the deal for John's head. None of these elements appear on screen, so a naive viewer would be puzzled as to what is going on. The beheading occurs off screen as Salome dances, Herod watches the dance, and John cries, "Repent. . ." Herod's next move, ultimately unfulfilled: "Now arrest the Nazarene."

The film makes clear that Jesus' primary opposition is from the house of Herod. The opposition is political, but also involves a theological position. The Herods believe that they can undo God's prophecy. They take a doomed position, in the context of the film, and as a result they fail.

In this drama John the Baptist constitutes the same bridge between old and new that he provides in the Gospels. He announces the coming of the Messiah. He preaches repentance before the coming wrath of God. By contrast, Jesus announces personal salvation and love, never retribution. When Herod's guards seek to arrest John he violently baptizes them, "I have orders to bring you to God, Heathen." John presents a robust, evangelical religion of repentance in anticipation of an angry God.

The character of John and his contrast with Jesus reveal two elements. Jesus is the New Covenant. He fulfills and regenerates the religion of the Old Covenant, which no longer has the power to awaken faith. He also represents the internal moral perfection of humans. The first element constitutes a modern retelling of the traditional Christian view of itself as the successor to Judaism as the chosen religion of God. The second element argues for modern American Protestantism to leave behind its evangelistic mission roots. Both views participate in the American view of steady progress of the individual through to the modern age.

Jesus, his disciples, or any other Jew are shown in the movie as being natural products of a realistically depicted Jewish culture. The film constructs historical verisimilitude sufficient for a somewhat "churched" American audience, but no more. It capitalizes on basic biblical literacy as did *King of Kings* (1927). From this literary understanding, it builds a picture of Judaism refracted through the American experience of frontier evangelism. This truly is a movie about the American Christ projected back to the origins of Christianity. While Jesus is supposed to be the timeless Logos, he represents the preferred American and Protestant future, which leaves behind its evangelical past.

Ultimately, the film proclaims a rather bald double successionism. Jesus displaces Old Testament faith including Judaism and Evangelicalism. Judas becomes the final impure sacrifice on an altar abandoned by God.

THE AUTHORITY OF ROME

The Romans play only a background role of grinding political authoritarianism in this film. In an early scene Jesus teaches his disciples beneath a bridge as Roman soldiers march over them. Pilate, the representative of Roman power, provides no real dramatic energy in opposition to Jesus. His wife's intervention makes little dramatic sense and seems to trouble Pilate not at all. He orders the suppression of a temple riot immediately after Jesus cleanses the temple. The scene evokes, perhaps, the future Christian persecution, but here the Roman response makes historical sense. If Jesus did cleanse the temple in Jerusalem, then the Roman response suppressing even the hint of a riot would have been swift and brutal. I might add that if Jesus did cleanse the temple as depicted in the Gospels, such an act would virtually guarantee that the Roman authorities would do everything they could to find him and eliminate him. Romans did not tolerate riots or breaches of public order in the temple or elsewhere.

THE MAKING OF THE AMERICAN CHRIST

The failure of *The Greatest Story Ever Told* is easy to attribute to the overambitious directing of George Stevens, but such a simple explanation may very well be unfair to a great director. Fox pulled out its financing early on, forcing Stevens to compromise his original vision. He cast known big-name actors in cameos to secure backing.[4] We should also bear in mind that some of the actors recognizable to us now were not big name actors at the time. Jamie Farr, later of *Mash* fame, and David McCallum, who was just beginning *The Man from Uncle* (1964), both fall into this category.

Expenses shot from $10 to $25 million, which for the early 1960s was fairly extreme. Multiple cuts that kept shortening the film also contribute to the film's lack of cohesion, especially in the postintermission portion.[5] Stevens may have been both ahead of and behind his time. Behind, because he shot a film even longer than *Spartacus* or *Ben-Hur* and with the same epic production values. Ahead, because it would not be until 1977 that Zeffirelli would convince NBC to invent the television mini-series for *Jesus of Nazareth*. Cut into smaller segments on successive nights on a television screen, *The Greatest Story Ever Told* plays very well (I suggest you try it).

Stevens' use of camera and technique really provides nothing new. The film uses an abundance of slow dissolves, long pull-outs, and slow pans. Stevens is master of the close-up; note particularly the scenes where Charlton Heston and Max Von Sydow appear together. He allows his actors wide latitude to develop their characters on screen. Any one scene develops as an artistic whole. Indeed the most enjoyable way to view the film is to watch selected best scenes and appreciate their composition and movement. This design cyclically layers the action, almost like a Van Gogh. For example, if we watch just the scenes involving Herod the Great and then Antipas his son we see repetitions of similar shots, action, and dialogue that by themselves contain a clear theological argument. Or watch only the scenes of John the Baptist and we can appreciate sharp acting and dramatic passion along with significant and exciting theological discussion. Jesus' scenes frequently lack the human emotion that would connect us viscerally to the story.

The film suggests real-time action, speeches, and reaction. See, for example, the Last Supper. The film avoids dwelling on the scourging or Via Dolorosa. This last, like Ray's film, is shot with the atmosphere of a respectful church service. The suffering, even on the cross, remains at a minimum. Scenes are intercut and crosscut to enhance drama. The Last Supper, Gethsemane, Trials, and Crucifixion gather together the elements of the Hollywood tradition. They become a template to be refilled by later directors.

Hollywood movies, like Americans and their faith, do not strive for authenticity, but for an appearance of historical verisimilitude. The techniques involved here derive once again from epics and Westerns. Contrary to Stevens' avowed interest in breaking new ground, the film remains well within if not trapped by the Cold War 1950s biblical spectacular. Like *King of Kings* (1961), the genre overwhelms Jesus. He simply does not achieve the agonized proportions anticipated for a great American hero. The film does not hang together as a dramatic whole primarily because Jesus is never allowed to communicate an emotional humanity.

The Greatest Story Ever Told arrives five years later than *King of Kings* (1961), therefore five years past the highpoint of epic films. It will be the last of the big-budget epics and will join films such as *Cleopatra* as box office disasters. The epic when it is revived will cease to be historical and will become transposed into sci-fi fantasy (*Star Wars*).

If Jesus is self-conscious of his identity with God from the beginning, he is not an easy subject for the audience to identify with and aspire to in the usual heroic mold. The author of the Gospel of John recognized this fact by adapting and creating a genre appropriate to the depiction of the incarnate God. John's Jesus does not bear the burden of being depicted as an epic hero as Stevens' does. There is no question of Jesus being a hero in John, nor is he absorbed into the heroic, agonistic model of Greco-Roman literature. America in its self-concept and conceit must be heroic. *The Greatest Story Ever Told* fails because it remains captive to the American need to see Jesus as itself, and yet it produces, despite the need of the audience and the conventions of the genre, a Christ that is more God than man.

Within the canonical Jesus tradition, the elements exist for a depiction of Jesus as a heroic apocalyptic prophet at war with the supernatural forces of evil (combine the Gospel of Mark with the Apocalypse of John). Since *The Greatest Story Ever Told* was bound by the assumption that its audience was the modern Protestant American mainstream, however, it could not be expected to exploit that particular trajectory. If anything, modern American Protestantism was profoundly uncomfortable with an apocalyptic Jesus, preferring instead an emphasis on Jesus as, in the film, a moral reformer of individuals. Mainstream film will remain unable to do this until the breakup of modern assumptions by the postmodern condition of late twentieth-century America. The process of demythologizing, reducing Jesus to supposedly rational and historical elements, continues to work full force in this film. An apocalyptic struggle with Satan remains out of the question. We must first go through the full existential self-examination of Jesus as man and strip him of his divine pretensions (the process of *Jesus Christ Superstar* and *The Last Temptation of Christ*) before he can reemerge heroically remythologized as an apocalyptic warrior in *The Passion of the Christ*.

The film assumes its more rightful place in this cinematic trajectory through the character of John the Baptist. The movie hopes to show, especially in those close-up two-shots between John and Jesus, the movement from a more primitive external transformation by conversion to a more internal ascent of the soul. The film thereby attempts to nostalgically relegate evangelical American religion to the frontier era. Charlton Heston, the quintessential American hero, defeats the film's intent. He presages the vigor of American evangelicalism as we will see it worked out in American culture and politics over the next four decades.

By the same token, the film's preference for an internalization of salvation will be de-Christianized and become commonplace in American film and culture. The development of that line of American spirituality in film can be seen as having been initiated by Stanley Kubrick's *2001: A Space Odyssey* (1968). Kubrick will achieve the theological move that *The Greatest Story Ever Told* sought. For *2001: A Space Odyssey* reworks the epic, dehistoricizes it and makes it a mythological backdrop for consideration of the ascent of the soul to higher consciousness. Alien intelligence substitutes for God, a monolith for the incarnate Logos.

The pathway taken by *2001: A Space Odyssey* depicts well the other approach to American religion in the late twentieth century. These two, the evangelical and the inward spiritual, also dominate the Jesus movies, with a strong infusion, as we shall see, of Catholic sacramentalism. *The Greatest Story Ever Told*, however, avoids any apocalyptic or eschatological interpretation of Jesus. Jesus is not an apocalyptic prophet who anticipates the coming judgment of the world by God. The film shows us no images of divine judgment. Even Jesus' cleansing of the temple, his most vigorous action in the movie, lacks an element of final judgment. The Crucifixion ends without any indication of judgment or apocalyptic portents, the ominous strictly atmospheric darkening of the sky notwithstanding. The temple veil is not torn on screen. A gentle, natural breeze blows it outward.

Satan appears as the exploiter of human frailty. He shows no supernatural powers befitting a prince of darkness. This continues a consistent view in Jesus films. In *King of Kings* (1927) he appears as a richly dressed handsome man, and in *King of Kings* (1961) only as a disembodied voice. Here he is a Dark Hermit, expressing the rationality of excessive human desires. In each case he expresses an externalization of America's fears about itself.

The modern American audience believes in the psychological approach; therefore, *The Greatest Story Ever Told* avoids showing nature miracles or demon possession. We see calm healings by faith. The battle here is not perceived as being cosmic, but as taking place within each individual. Judas now shows no signs of greed, nor political ambition. He makes a bad choice.

The landscape in *The Greatest Story Ever Told* inserts America into the Christ myth. The Christ is the divine consciousness distributed over the American desert. His resurrection indicates the apotheosis of a new and unified America—an apolitical America, unified instead by the spirit. From the desert of our souls will come forth spiritual abundance. The time of material and political struggle has past.

While the dramatic action of *The Greatest Story Ever Told* fails to carry us all the way along to its final message, the film does expose its connections to an American mythology. By avoiding history, the director can avoid a genuine confrontation with American anti-Semitism. *The Greatest Story Ever Told* masks an evolutionary view in which Judaism is absorbed and rendered unidentifiable by the American mainstream. The film advocates the ideal of individual inner change as the best avenue for the transformation of society. Each person becomes America. Each contains the Christ who embodies the future of America, who is all of humanity. Ultimately this view indicates a unified but nevertheless Christian cultural consciousness.

All three of the movies treated so far share the intent to unite the audience within a common (Protestant) master narrative. The audience ideally knows the truth of the myth of America as the story of Christ for itself and for the world. But *The Greatest Story Ever Told* will be the last mainstream Jesus film to presume and strive for this audience unity. The films to come will divide their audience. In addition, Catholics will direct all but one of those that remain for our consideration. What *The Greatest Story Ever Told* contains in its specific time capsule is the exhaustion of modern liberal Protestant mainstream America. After this, Jesus film, like America, divides culturally into two camps; the remaining films construct their audience on one side or the other of a great divide.

Hollywood film at its root remains tied to Christian assumptions. While the split of audience has regularly been seen as a split between American secularism and religion, the reality is that American audiences and films are almost uniformly Christian in their mythologies. The battle appears when the identification of mythic polarities and their resolutions into cultural norms are in conflict. Where, on a surface reading, Hollywood-produced or distributed films are not about Christianity, they always absorb even foreign religious and mythic elements into an American, which is to say Christian, model. Like Judah Ben-Hur, all heroes are allowed to revenge themselves, but then must convert.

The failure of *The Greatest Story Ever Told* is not in its acting, directing, or cinematography. The failure is its appeal to a unifying Protestant experience of self at a time when, unrecognized by most, that experience was already crumbling. Successful films might nostalgically appeal to that narration, but the rebirth of the heroic epic will require a recasting of the historical epic into a new guise manifested first in science fantasy. Jesus films will now take another turn and explore different genres that allow the construction of Jesus as a hero.

4

JESUS CHRIST SUPERSTAR:
THE CINEMATIC SAVIOR AS
ALIENATED HERO

THE COUNTERCULTURE HERO

In order to make Jesus heroic, we must first make him human. To be human in 1960s America meant alienation, self-doubt, and the dramatic exploration of self, standing on the verge of new creation. *Jesus Christ Superstar* presents a very human Jesus in a new musical form that allows repeated self-exploration as the spirituality of the 1960s found its most striking expression in the music of the era. His journey as always is the American journey, but most of the cast and the cinematic audience are taking it "on the bus."

With *Jesus Christ Superstar*, Jesus no longer belongs to the church. His reformation on screen as a satisfying American hero depended upon American culture's ongoing shift in religion. This shift is one that has been popularly characterized as the secularization of America. But the shift was not simply a rejection of the religious for the secular, but rather involved a subtle process of change and interpretation in American religion. In the United States, religion has tended to carry identification with church or congregation membership, and a simplistic dichotomy developed in the popular imagination: A person was either churchgoing or secular. From the 1960s forward, the power of the mainstream Protestant consensus increasingly fragmented and evaporated from American public life. We have already seen some evidence of this in *The Greatest Story Ever Told* and even *King of Kings* (1961). Christian equaled churchgoer, and in the popular media, this generally came to mean Evangelical Protestants and Roman Catholics. The remainder of America is secular, or when attacked from the traditionals' point of view, leftist, liberal, God-denying.

If we are to understand the Cinematic Savior, however, we need to recognize that he is a product of American religious culture, even though he no longer exists as the canonical icon of the church or churches exclusively. He belongs to the mythological symbol set that all Americans use to express their own religious or spiritual experience. When the Protestant consensus came apart, the result was not a Godless or Christless America; instead the Christ moved from church control to a popular and perhaps more adaptable savior. He carried with him traditional associations, and he acquired a new heroic status. Jesus became human and more recognizably like us. In contrast to *The Greatest Story Ever Told*, his conflict became more human. We can view with close precision just when this transformation takes place in the Cinematic Savior through the phenomenon of *Jesus Christ Superstar*.

The shift from the historical epic to rock opera, a new performance genre, allowed the remythologizing of Jesus as a universal savior to take place. *Jesus Christ Superstar* places Jesus in the middle of contemporary American culture with no attempt at a reproduction of the ancient context of Jesus himself, as in biblical spectaculars.

The most obvious bridge for the audience is the genre itself; rock and roll was invented by the younger generation for the younger generation. It represents their voice, their very being, even their soul, whose existence remains a question. The film plays exclusively to that young audience of spiritual seekers with little regard for mainstream sensibilities. Like the musical culture out of which it arises, the movie represents a clear choice about the future of America. It leaves behind the Establishment, which it regards as corrupt and self-interested. It seeks authentic existence.

While historical epic or biblical spectacular no longer dominates the form, sex, sadism, and melodrama remain. *Jesus Christ Superstar* returns to the love triangle of Judas, Jesus, and Magdalene introduced by DeMille. Jesus, however, becomes for the first time an American hero complete with temptation and doubt. He is pressed realistically by his humanity (Does he sleep with Magdalene? Will he go to the cross?). He nevertheless remains true to divine will no matter how impenetrable it may appear to be for him. These two components of heroic self-sacrifice, essential to Hollywood heroes—the necessity of choice within a framework of uncertainty—now become absorbed into the Cinematic Savior.

Jesus Christ Superstar focuses the audience's attention on the physical and psychological anguish, and Hollywood subsequently adopts this theological lens through which the Cinematic Savior appears. An uncertain America projects its heroic self onto an impenetrable future. The underlying anxiety seems to be about our theological mandates.

The Love Triangle Again

The first character to appear on screen, Judas establishes the perspective for the movie. Judas, cast as a black man, states the problem: The Jesus movement, which had been a reform movement initially, has gotten out of hand, "We must keep in our place. . . . We are occupied, have you forgotten how put down we are?" Concentration on the things of heaven will lead to our destruction. Jesus has become the subject and object of devotion. Judas sees the danger of Jesus as the Christ, the Son of God. Judas fears the Romans; he cringes at martyrdom. He also dislikes hero worship, and Jesus is on the way to becoming a superstar with illusions of divine status. As we discover in his next song, Judas also disapproves of the sexual relationship between Jesus and Magdalene. From the first scene of the film, these three motives provide the grounds for Judas's betrayal.

Judas fails to understand the inconsistencies in Jesus' behavior as death approaches. He becomes convinced that Jesus wants to die and comes to see his own role as helping that to happen. As with Jesus, a divine will surrounds and traps Judas. We follow his steady and inevitable deterioration into betrayal and suicide. His misunderstanding of Jesus signifies the spiritual confusion of America. Judas seems to dominate Jesus in the film. For the first time in Hollywood history the audience sees Jesus from the perspective of Judas, from "Heaven on Their Minds" to the climactic "Superstar." Judas's questions of Jesus, his mission, his decision to die, become prompts for audience reflection. Is Jesus human? What did Jesus think of his own mission? Is there God, and salvation?

The movie presents Judas as an iconographic opposite to Jesus. He is black; Jesus is white. He dresses in red, Jesus in white. They are also musically contrasted. Judas, arguably, has the better voice and delivers more powerful vocals. Jesus is tired, at times on the verge of vocal collapse. Judas's devolution into the role of betrayer begins early with "Strange Thing Mystifying." He accuses Magdalene of wasting precious ointment. His concern is only for the poor. Judas criticizes Jesus' dalliance with Magdalene. He delivers Jesus to Caiaphas and the Sanhedrin. He hangs himself; Jesus is hung on the cross. The struggle is between Jesus and Judas. God stands above and beyond, compelling the struggle but never making an appearance.

Jesus Christ Superstar pictures Judas as morally upright, a true believer in the cause, never as avaricious or power hungry. We move forward with Judas in the desert. Pleasant, pastoral music accompanies him as tanks begin to roll in behind, and eventually reality overtakes the reverie. The horror of the juxtaposition references perhaps the use of Wagner's "Ride of the Valkyries," in *Apocalypse Now*. The militarism of the tanks provides the backdrop to Judas's betrayal. But the tanks symbolize not ancient Rome but contemporary America.

Judas has the omniscience of an operatic character and can comment on his own future reputation. In "Damned for All Time" he addresses the audience directly. The film continues to build the American film tradition that sees Judas as a tragic character, misled by the best of intentions. He does not betray Jesus of his "own accord." He rejects "blood money." He desires exoneration. He, like Jesus, finds himself trapped by divine will.

Jesus explores his own humanity in the face of inevitable death according to divine plan. He musically balances the role of Judas. His vocals are always defensive of his choices or corrective of misunderstandings. He defends his relationship to Magdalene by allusion to the scene of the stoning of an unknown woman found in John 8: "If your slate is clean, then you can throw stones . . . "

Later, Jesus corrects the enthusiasm of Simon Zealotes; no one, including crowds, Romans, Jews, Judas, nor the Twelve, understands, "To conquer death you only have to die." At this point in the plot, before Gethsemane, Jesus expresses no confusion about his mission or fate.

Jesus Christ Superstar explores the psychological and emotional side of Jesus as he approaches his death. In doing so it creates opportunities for interpretations only indirectly explored or left unexplored by the Gospels and the church. Among the Gospels that of Mark comes closest to the approach of the film. Mark leaves the reader fleeing with the women from the empty tomb (16:8), a situation that made later readers so unsettled that some second-century scribes tried to add new endings (Mark 16:9–20). Mark contains no Resurrection, but only Crucifixion. More important, like the style of this film, Mark's style is highly paratactic, meaning that each paragraph or scene in Mark occurs without clear syntactical relationship to the previous scene or vignette. Each Markan story stands alone. Only the placement of each piece allows the reader guidance as to how to relate each scene from the life of Jesus to the others.

Film, and particularly this film, works the same way. The audience views scene sequence, but with little guidance as to how to connect the sequence meaningfully. The underlying meaning of Jesus' action remains unexplored directly by the Markan narrator, or in the film, by the camera. The viewer deciphers the meaning from clues in the film. Mark leaves the audience with, "My God, My God, why have you forsaken me?" as the last words uttered by Jesus. Mark leaves it to the reader to decide in what psychological state Jesus died.

By adopting the form of opera, by providing no discursive interpretative narrative from one song to the next, *Jesus Christ Superstar* gives a similar freedom to the audience. That Jesus' faith is tested becomes apparent first in the single scene of healings. The choreography, modern and evocative of Martha Graham, shows the struggle of Jesus' own fatigue in the face of incessant, pitiable cries for healing. The scene becomes surreal. Martin Scorsese will use the scene again in *The Last Temptation of Christ*. Jesus, near the end, appears to lack the power to heal.

Jesus Christ Superstar suggests that after three years of devotion, the mission exhausts Jesus of his power. His struggle becomes real. In "Gethsemane" Jesus directly questions God. His disciples are drunk and sleeping. In a dramatic duet with Jesus, Judas deserts him to betray. Jesus' prayer-ballad to God borrows from Mark 14:32–42. Jesus prays for the cup to be taken away, as "surely I've exceeded expectations. . . .Show me just a little of your omnipresent brain."

By allowing Jesus to raise the possibility of doubt, fatigue, and alienation, *Jesus Christ Superstar* achieves a human and heroic characterization that is missing from previous movies. Tempted like us, he decides to submit to the will of God even though no direct answer comes back. "Bleed me, beat me, kill me, take me now—before I change my mind." The low to high camera shot connecting earth to heaven, Jesus to God, places the audience within the mythical axis along which heavenly knowledge comes. The film evokes God, never doubts God's presence by the pregnant contrast of high and low shots, through which the earthly–heavenly axis of myth comes into visual reality.

After, "Show me just a little of your omnipresent brain," the film cuts from Jesus to 23 shots of Crucifixion art in 26 seconds.[1] The rapid acceleration of pace could be God's revelation to Jesus; certainly, it is the film's reminder to the audience of the horrible death that awaits him and its denouement throughout subsequent Christian artistic history. The scene places us in the position of both Jesus and God. Would we die in order to consummate this future? Jesus does.

Any interpretation of *Jesus Christ Superstar* must reckon with the clear implication that Jesus knows his death, along with its later interpretations, and goes willingly to it. In creating sequential images that enfold the audience in the drama, film does here what it does best. Unlike Hitchcock, Lewison here breaks through the filmic window, what on a stage would be called the "fourth wall." He relentlessly forces the audience from voyeurism to participation.

We become part of Jesus' deciding. In Gethsemane, he ceases to be an icon and becomes a fully realized human hero. The immediate dissolve to

Judas connects Jesus' resolve to embrace the will of an unknowable God with Judas's betrayal. Judas will be saved by Jesus' decision.

Before turning to that resolution, however, we need to analyze the third member of the triangle, Magdalene. *Jesus Christ Superstar* updates DeMille's formula of sex, sadism, and melodrama. The updating results in a different interpretation of Magdalene as Ur-woman, or earth mother, Eve. She is no longer a courtesan who aspires to wealth and power but rather a sexually experienced woman (the film never calls her a prostitute) who loves Jesus and wants him as lover. The film, unlike some stage productions, leaves open the question as to whether she consummates the relationship with Jesus. Judas obviously regards their relationship as inappropriate. The other apostles, who are not depicted as ascetics but as part of a mixed band of male and female disciples, show no disapproval.

Magdalene, like Judas, is characterized by the red of her clothing. Continuing the use of the vertical axis, the camera shows us the disciple band in an underground cave. Magdalene holds Jesus' head in her lap, a transference of the pieta motif in Christian art; here, though, Magdalene takes on the role of the Mother of Jesus. She now becomes the Mother, incorporating Mary and overtones of earth goddesses like Demeter. This representation establishes contact with traditional pre-Christian images of sexuality and fertility. Jesus and Magdalene in this scene visually construct a divine couple surrounded by their own holy family.

Visually, iconically, filmically, the film reincorporates positive images of sexuality, comfort, and the feminine that were lost or suppressed in the history of American Christianity. Unlike *The Last Temptation of Christ,* in which Jesus is tortured by questions of body and spirit, woman and man, *Jesus Christ Superstar* implies a Jesus unified in body and spirit. He is not fractured by asceticism. And in fact the movie damned itself for a large section of the American public by suggesting that the Christ is an integrated sexual human.

Unlike the previous Jesus films, in *Jesus Christ Superstar* Magdalene is not saved from her sin; she does not convert. Rather, she seems transformed or transposed. She expresses her confusion in the middle of this process of self-realization in the ballad "I Don't Know How to Love Him." There she recognizes Jesus' humanity, "he's just one more," and his otherness, "he scares me so." The effectiveness of the scene depends on the human desire to be seen as equal to, yet different from, the heroic other. We are both part of a family, a mythically grounded society, as well as called to overcome our own alienation in formulating with others a positive society. Magdalene in *Jesus Christ Superstar* shows the need to reintegrate the feminine into the Christian and American mythos. We will find it in other forms—updated, for example, when we look at *The Matrix.*

Mary's own transformation occurs during a duet with Peter, "Start Again Please," written exclusively for the film. Compared with the previous film tradition of Magdalene, the scene lacks a dramatic conversion from promiscuity to chastity. She does not don a nun's habit or veil. She remains Earth Mother or wife-consort. She does want to start again, but without denying anything in her experience. She acquires a new beginning with Peter that is signified by a new white garment. Since she is never a "sinner woman" except in Judas's eyes, she cannot be perceived in the context of the film as a fallen woman. Unless of course we adopt Judas's mistaken point of view.

SADISTS ON THE SCENE

Sadism arrives in the persons of Herod and Pilate. In this rendition, sadism is the special purview of gay culture. The tradition is quite old in Hollywood stereotypes. Reaching back to DeMille's *Sign of the Cross* (1932) and continuing through Stanley Kubrick's *Spartacus* (1960), lurid homosexuality has been used to type the ruling class. Charles Laughton's extremely fey bi- or homosexual Nero in *Sign of the Cross* sets the stage for the lurid sadism and homoeroticism that recurs throughout the movie. Or we can recall the homosexual designs of Lawrence Olivier's Crassus on his slave Antoninus, played by Tony Curtis in *Spartacus*, that eventually drive Antoninus to seek refuge with Spartacus. Here in *Jesus Christ Superstar*, Herod appears as what now looks like a proto-Boy George, floating with his boys and girls atop the Dead Sea and demanding miracles before sending a silent Jesus back to Pilate.

Pilate himself enters as an English homosexual aristocrat who is so aroused (along with Herod) by the power struggle with Jesus that the subsequent scourging brings them both almost to orgasmic release. Certainly the women, presumably their wives, receive no such sexual attention from either. The stereotype that sadism is the territory of queers and aristocrats aligns *Jesus Christ Superstar* with a Hollywood tradition that continues to the present day. Underlying it may be the association in American film of the British with the Romans and both with homosexuals. These are imperialists who oppress and torture honest American manhood.

Caiaphas, Annas, the Sanhedrin: Anti-Semitism in *Jesus Christ Superstar?*

In terms of visual iconography, the staged surreal quality and the multiethnic cast allow *Jesus Christ Superstar* to move beyond Hollywood's stereotyped patterns of casting to a theatrical, universal level. To represent Judas and Simon Zealotes as African American or to equip Caiaphas, Annas, and the Sanhedrin with black capes, leather headgear, and scaffolding says little directly about betrayal or responsibility for Jesus' death, unless the viewer brings such prejudices directly to the movie. According to the film, African Americans and Jews are not responsible for Jesus' death.

Although this film emphasizes and re-emphasizes the fact of Roman military occupation, the Sanhedrin assumes the larger and more theatrical role in Jesus' condemnation. If the Sanhedrin is guilty, in no way are they represented as "the Jews." If you are on the bus, you know it is "The Man," "The Establishment." Remember that Watergate broke the year the movie was released. Kent State happened two years earlier. The temple, for example, no longer represents the ancient Jewish religious site, but the modern American marketplace. You can buy everything from postcards to prostitutes to guns. When Jesus cleanses the temple, he cleanses America of its vices as a nation.

Neither *King of Kings (1927)* nor *The Greatest Story Ever Told* achieves clear analogues between ancient history and the contemporary corruption of the American spirit. They, perhaps, do not take seriously institutional parallels between the ancient and modern situation. *Jesus Christ Superstar* abandons any attempt at depicting ancient culture and thereby contemporizes Christ as responding to the specific vices of America. In short, Jesus saves America from the commercialization of war, sex, and drugs that enriches her. They, as the religious establishment (transparently the churches of America), support the imperialism of Rome (transparently Washington) out of fear and desire for power. Like ravens on a battlefield, they pick off the souls of humans after the tanks have ground them under. It is difficult not to read here the open street warfare between the counterculture and the American government from the antiwar protests at the University of Michigan through the Kent State killings. *Jesus Christ Superstar* is a passion play about the American Christ crucified by the American establishment. Jesus' rage and the film's perspective are directed against the abuses of the American governmental and religious establishment. So when Jesus, the American Christ, cleanses the temple it is America seeking to cleanse itself.

Such elements do not undercut the theological legitimacy of the film, since the film nowhere leads the audience to believe that an authentic rendition of the historical Jesus is its object. As we have seen, the very nature of its presentation stands starkly against such an interpretation. *Jesus Christ Superstar*, more than any previous Jesus film, perceives God as present in the so-called secular realm. The division of America into church and state, sacred and profane, or pious and secular obscures the reality of American self-perception and, more importantly, practice. *Jesus Christ Superstar* shows us an American cultural response that remythologizes and resacramentalizes American life where modernity had attempted to rationalize and historicize it. In doing so, it denies the validity of a secular/sacral society that allows for abuses in the name of God. For example, by heroizing Jesus as the purifier of religious/profane America of its war-for-profit trade, the movie suggests that Jesus can stand against the society that worships him, but refuses to follow him. Only in this movie can Jesus say that no one "understands at all." His message stands against America, not Rome, nor the Jews, nor foreigners. He preaches and acts against us, whether we are counterculture, like Peter, or imperialists, like Rome, or anyone in between.

Far from signaling a loss of God, the real opposition created within the film is between all of a faithless America and God. Both Jesus and Judas believe to the end. The pathway remains with the sheep on the hillside, not in the withdrawal to the psychedelic road trip of the bus.

HOLLYWOOD'S MAKING OF THE AMERICAN CHRIST: THEOLOGICAL AND MYTHOLOGICAL REVERSALS

At its center, theologically and mythologically, *Jesus Christ Superstar* reverses the Hollywood and canonical expectations of Jesus. Mary is not fallen; she simply requires transposition to new levels of spiritual awareness. Judas is not greedy, jealous, or possessed by Satan; he is a mistaken, if cowardly, moralist. Jesus, while omniscient ("I wonder how he knew"), makes a human and heroic choice to place himself in the hands of an impenetrable God.

The reversal from traditional American and Christian theology underlies the film's offensiveness for many viewers of *Jesus Christ Superstar*: God becomes genuine mystery known only to God's self and unavailable to human control. Even Jesus' omniscience cannot penetrate to God. The character of God lurks behind and above every scene, as question. The film evokes God as a question and makes God even more impenetrable through its cinematography, its perspective. As we have already seen at Gethsemane, the movement between low and high shots reflects the exploration of the relationship between Jesus and God. The camera never doubts the reality of God. The same can be said of Judas and Mary in their key scenes. If *Jesus Christ Superstar* exploits a romantic triangle for sexual energy and drama, it ultimately does so in order to raise significant questions about traditional American views of God, especially the view that we can discern God's meaning and purposes for us.

In *Jesus Christ Superstar* God comes into the film more than in any previous mainstream film. *Jesus Christ Superstar* resacramentalizes the tradition that previous films attempted to demythify out of a dominant cultural unease with the supernatural or real presence of God in history and nature. The vertical visual axis repeated almost scene by scene recurs to evoke mythological effect. In this, the film must be seen on its own, without reference to stage production or rock album, because only in film can the camera control the visual experience of the audience. Only in film is "point of view" truly controlled by the literal visual nature of the medium.

Jesus Christ Superstar denotes the split of Americans into two general religious streams. One, the traditional, composed of Evangelicals and Catholics, increasingly sees itself as the conservers of the only true Christian and American religion. From the point of view of the Cinematic Savior, traditionals hold in common a canonical, theological view of Jesus. Jesus is God, unwaveringly. For them *Jesus Christ Superstar* is a blatant misrepresentation of Jesus by the "secular" artistic community.

In contrast to this characterization, the second stream can be seen as no less Christian and no less American in its mythology or spiritual sensibilities and theological structures. From that perspective Jesus is seen as a heroic individual for whom the question of God is open and who leads toward new exploration of the self or soul with no clear answers. The primary image of ascent toward God comes not only visually but musically. The use of rock and opera allows for a re-incorporation of feelings of alienation from God as part of faith. It grounds that faith in a musical form that liberates emotion, and thus as well the sexual and spiritual. Interestingly enough, rock has a part of its roots in the hymns exploited by DeMille. Unlike the later and more conventional *The Last Temptation of Christ*, the problem here is not simply the classical conundrum of God in a body, but the social and cultural issue of humanity's bodily relationship to God. The classic Protestant solution was to remove the historical world as secular from the divine sphere as holy and treat the secular as dead matter to be engaged ascetically. While Catholicism also treated the necessity of removal of the spiritual from the world, perhaps it also maintained a more intimate view of the sacramental presence of God in the world.[2] In this sense, *Jesus Christ Superstar* denotes the beginning of a more "catholic" sensibility in American film. Subsequent films will give dominance to this sensibility.

Admittedly, this interpretation depends on an empathetic read of the climactic scene. Unlike the vision of *The Last Temptation of Christ*, however, its placement and staging suggest multiple perspectives of revelation for the audience to consider: those of Jesus, Judas, and our own. Within the film, it occurs during/after Jesus' scourging, and after Pilate condemns him to death as a "misguided puppet." It is the revelatory moment from heaven to the audience about the meaning of the American Christ, primarily because it is not shot through Jesus' eyes, but in the light of a cold third-person window through which the audience may view the heavenly vision. Heaven opens to us. We know what God is willing to reveal.

Prior to this scene, Judas dies convinced of his infamy and of Jesus' innocence. He murders an innocent man, who is just a man. He doesn't know how to love him. He prays to God. He is unjustly lynched by his own hand, behind which stands the religious establishment, which also conspires to eliminate the Christ. The death scene of Judas, a black man at the end of a rope from a low angle, evokes historical scenes of lynching in America. In American film tradition the lynched man is always innocent.[3] The self-lynching of Judas signifies, then, his innocence to the audience. Judas, the ultimate symbol of evil in Christendom becomes in *Jesus Christ Superstar* the lynched black man at the end of the white man's rope. His self-inflicted death becomes murder at the hands the Establishment's God, "You have murdered me." With him dies, figuratively, the projected view of the White God as a just God. The target of the savage critique is the contemporary American religious establishment, not the unknowable, true God of Jesus.

Jesus Christ Superstar destabilizes and overturns American religious prejudices, especially our own sense of perfectibility. Judas, as the climactic "Superstar" scene shows, does not go to Dante's final ring of hell, but rather to heaven. Judas has ascended into the heavens, saved by an unknown God. Yet he bears no new revelation, "Every time I look at you I don't understand . . . If you'd come today you would have reached a whole nation, Israel in 4 B.C. had no mass communication." Or, as *King of Kings* (1927) claimed, now with the universal availability of American film, we will save the world for Christ and Capitalism. His song ironically suggests that even with our modern advantages we still would not have believed, and we would have crucified the very Lord we now worship. Judas has been to heaven, which is where we expect revelation of God's purposes for America. He descends from the heavens clothed in white fringe, suggesting angel's wings. He, and we, still don't get it.

Further, a globally aware American audience wants to know God's view of world religions, but Judas hasn't a clue: "Buddha was he where it's at? Is he where you are? Could Mohammed move a mountain or was that just P.R.?" Judas keenly addresses the two major competitors on the horizon against Christianity for the souls of America in 1973. Jesus, Judas, and God have no answer. The audience must resolve the questions for itself guided only by Jesus' own heroic faith.

The implication, unpalatable to traditional Christian theology, is that either God does not know or does not choose to reveal his own truth. Faith must be an uncertain leap, not a commodified package, with money-back guaranteed. Latent is the presumption that everyone knows, theology aside, that Christianity as a national movement has failed its Savior repeatedly. The movie addresses directly a crisis of faith for the American religious experience. As a progressive force, history proves the Christian claims about God and Jesus wrong. None can claim that by any historical measure Jesus was successful. We have not fulfilled the promise of Christ's message of love for neighbor and care for the poor in 2,000 years of Christian history, nor in 200 years of American. Is faith possible anyway? The point of the scene is to call to mind Jesus' future, our past, and the mainstream aspirations of American religion whether Protestant liberal, Evangelical, or Catholic.

Jesus Christ Superstar leaves us with the Crucifixion as tragic denouement to the climactic, revelatory scene. Unlike the Gospel of Mark in chapter 13, Jesus has no vision of the end of time and the gathering of the elect. With homage to DeMille, we see briefly the Via Dolorosa. An homage to Ray provides a view from the top of the cross. Jesus utters five of the canonical statements from the cross, "Forgive them . . . Why have you forgotten me? . . . I am thirsty . . . It is finished . . . Into your hands . . . " In *Jesus Christ Superstar* Magdalene absorbs the function of Mary the Mother, who makes no appearance at the cross, nor in the movie.

Rather than a climax, the cross becomes a stark beginning of a denouement that carries us back to the opera within the movie. We get back on the bus. By adopting the form of opera, *Jesus Christ Superstar* exploits both melodrama and music as a means to reconfigure the Cinematic Savior tradition. The artifice of theatrical production is exposed to the audience by the opening and closing scenes. The actors arrive on a bus, with cross on top. As they get off the bus, we are introduced to the cast. But, we never see Jesus (Ted Neely) get off the bus. He appears first emerging from a circle of worshipful dancers as Jesus Christ Superstar. The audience knows it enters not into a world of authenticity, but of theatrical artifice. We know we are in the constructed world of interpretation.

The symbol of "the bus" could not be lost on an American audience in 1973, at least the preferred, target audience of the movie. The symbol of "being on the bus" signifies the countercultural experience of spiritual subversion of the 1960s. The idea was fixed by Ken Kesey's psychedelic bus trip to the New York World's fair in 1964, conceived and executed as a symbolic, sacramental act in confrontation with triumphant American modernity. Tom Wolfe later immortalized the trip and the movement in *The Electric Kool-Aid Acid Test*.[4] We know what it means to be on the bus, to be in, to know the real truth behind appearances, to have direct unmediated insight. It is a position of existing, not existence.

When, therefore, at the end everyone returns to the bus, without dancing or singing, what does it mean that Jesus is not there? The cross remains on the hill; it does not get back on the bus. In the foreground we see the silhouette of a shepherd leading his sheep. The shepherd has appeared earlier in the movie, so it may be too facile to see Jesus in the shepherd, although that is a natural reading of the symbol. The question of Resurrection remains unresolved.

Or does it? Jesus never got off the bus; he never gets on the bus. Christ cannot be the exclusive possession of either group, those on or those off. By its ambiguity, the film constructs a Christ outside of the control of church iconography or subversive iconoclasm. Potential for the reappearance of the Christ remains the possession of the supernatural (in this case nonmovie) realm. Much like the Gospel of Mark, which originally ended with 16:8, only God determines the revelation of Resurrection.

The Christ cannot be themed, institutionalized, nor claimed for any movement. The film deftly refuses to allow any single group to claim Christ and through him, God, as their own personally constructed Lord, Savior, Wiseman, Guru, or Martyr-Hero. This is the only American Jesus film to refuse to make an identification between the Christ and America. In it Christ, who is represented as so American, cannot finally be America.

Most important for Jesus films, however, Jesus, despite the exploration of Judas, remains the hero. *Jesus Christ Superstar* finally introduces Jesus as hero into the Hollywood tradition. By emphasizing his humanity with elements of doubt, fatigue, and despair left unresolved and intact through the end, *Jesus Christ Superstar* provides the basis for the heroizing of Jesus in later films. Jesus really, dramatically, suffers and doubts. The real possibility for unfaith is there. Therefore, his death is shown as a willing acceptance of what he does not understand.

Faced with an unsure future, America can conceive of itself as dedicated to high ethical ideas even if it cannot see the outcome. Without the move accomplished by *Jesus Christ Superstar,* neither Scorsese's nor Gibson's interpretations could have emerged from the tradition. From here forward Hollywood will not produce an American Christ bounded by the traditions of Gospels and church. Rather, from this movie forward Hollywood will primarily be referencing its own heroic tradition when constructing the Christ.

5

JESUS OF NAZARETH: THE CONTRIBUTION OF TELEVISION

THE NEW TRADITIONAL CINEMATIC SAVIOR

The last chapter concluded with the observation that Hollywood after *Jesus Christ Superstar* does not produce an American Christ controlled by the traditions of the Gospels and church. This does not, mean, however, that Hollywood does not bring out a new canonical Christ who appeals to a broad cross section of what we have called traditionals composed primarily of Evangelicals and Roman Catholics. The remarkable development in Hollywood and also American religious history generally is that the demise of church control of film nevertheless produces a highly traditional Jesus who belongs to America as surely as the Jesus of *Jesus Christ Superstar.*

The Italian Franco Zeffirelli directs the miniseries *Jesus of Nazareth,* which becomes the canon that defines Jesus for recent popular and especially traditional imagination. It was the first made-for-TV miniseries and re-airs yearly at Easter. It also is the first American production directed by a Catholic—all of our previous movies were directed by Protestants. Zeffirelli's artistic attempts to produce screen icons worthy of contemplation and worship by the faithful represents a shift in American representations of Jesus toward classic renaissance and medieval church art with extensive reflection on the Passion. Its most interesting plot aspect is the explanation of the betrayal by Judas: A political advisor to the high priest dupes him.

Jesus of Nazareth represents a return to the classic Cinematic Savior tradition of Hollywood found in the works of DeMille, Ray, and Stevens, ignoring the innovations of *Jesus Christ Superstar*. Thereby it appeals almost nostalgically to an earlier Jesus and promotes him to dominating status by the use of the first TV miniseries.

In *Jesus of Nazareth* we find no romantic triangles. What sex, sadism, or melodrama of the DeMille formula that we see is limited to subsidiary characters, primarily the household of Herod, which has by this time become a Hollywood cliché. According to Hollywood, the Herodians suffer every imaginable corruption of sex and power.

In a book limited to a consideration of Hollywood's making of the Cinematic Savior, the inclusion of the first six-hour television miniseries originally conceived as a joint Italian and British production requires some explanation. When the project was sold to NBC, they invented the miniseries format exclusively for this film. Zeffirelli shot the series intending it to be released on television, and he fully utilizes the potentials of the medium. The dimensions of the television screen, approximating as it does the old "snap-shot" dimensions of a Kodak camera, allow for an intimacy of presentation and a seamlessness of story. *Jesus of Nazareth* contains hardly a bad shot. Each scene is a stand-alone, didactic vignette. The six-hour time-frame allows a full exploration of the story of Jesus. The series format allows not only the inclusion of a huge amount of familiar Jesus episodes derived from the Gospels, but also allows for creative construction of interpretation and explanation. The verisimilitude of the production is enhanced. It explains everything.

By being made for television, *Jesus of Nazareth* appeals not to the avant-garde but to the broader American public. Its continued rebroadcast at Easter places its images at the level of popular tradition. If *Jesus Christ Superstar* was the initiation of the nontraditional investigation of Jesus in American movies, then *Jesus of Nazareth* canonizes the emergent traditional conception. By forging a moderate Cinematic Savior that appeals to people of both Protestant and Catholic backgrounds, it erases the traditional enmity between the established and largely immigrant American communities in a manner that would have been unthinkable when *King of Kings* (1961) or *The Greatest Story Ever Told* (1965) was produced. It also manages to mute the images of the Gospel tradition that had been regularly interpreted as anti-Semitic. *Jesus of Nazareth* merges Protestant and Catholic iconic traditions. Without its cinematic and theological innovations neither the Savior of *The Last Temptation of Christ* nor of *The Passion of the Christ* would have been able to emerge.

THE TRILOGY OF *JESUS OF NAZARETH*

Jesus of Nazareth, while originally shown in America on two consecutive Sundays (finishing on Easter, 1977), structurally contains three segments that almost constitute three distinct and individual films.[1] They interlock to form a trilogy of Jesus' life, not unlike the recent film trilogies of *The Matrix* or *Lord of the Rings*. Part one introduces Jesus' earthly family, concluding with the healing of a demoniac in a synagogue in Galilee. Part two centers on the call of the disciples and the public ministry of Jesus, concluding with the raising of Lazarus. Part three is the Passion and Resurrection narrative. A dramatic miracle punctuates the climax of each part.

Unlike previous film productions, melodrama is largely absent from the main storyline. Jesus remains unquestionably divine and so far above the fray that an existential or authentic exploration of human doubt is out of the question. He is in command of himself and his mission throughout. Nevertheless, the divine and human elements of his personality function smoothly together, as is shown by long scenes of Jesus' storytelling or teaching. This Jesus has humor and charismatic appeal. He is not so ethereal that he appears out of touch with real human life. The lengthened format aids in this characterization by also allowing the film to construct the society in which Jesus dwells. The film develops its own culture of Judaism, thereby enhancing a realistic or authentic feel to the film and to Jesus' life. We should not mistake it for an historical reconstruction of that society or life, however. Rather, its vignettes, mise-en-scene, and especially its cinematography, which evokes great church art, establish an iconography that feels right. The audience can relate to the film in a contemplative if not worshipful manner. The film manages to include the anticipations and prejudices of the audience while also revealing something new about Jesus.

The length of the film allows for the inclusion of almost every Gospel episode of the life of Jesus, but the viewer does not need a detailed knowledge of the Bible to understand Jesus. Most important, the audience need not keep careful track from scene to scene; rather each scene is a complete, intimate teaching moment in itself. The film also includes a large amount of interpretative and explanatory material that seamlessly connects each scene. This leaves viewers with the impression that they are looking at the complete history of Jesus. If the viewer is conscious of the contents of the Gospels, their variations are explained as versions of the greater life. The impression and reconstruction is compelling and not unlike what historians have attempted in writing the life of Jesus. Unlike the task of the historian, however, the test of a television production is its dramatic viability, not its historical accuracy.

A major problem for harmonizing the four different Gospels is that each has a different understanding of Jesus' own messianic consciousness. In Matthew and Mark, and to a lesser extent Luke, Jesus tends to keep his identity as the Son of God a secret for a significant part of his ministry. When they are compared to John, where Jesus openly proclaims himself Son of God from the beginning of his ministry to the end, the critical interpreter of all four Gospels is faced with a difficult problem: Did Jesus advocate himself as a secret or open messiah? The film solves this problem dramatically by having Jesus proclaim himself openly as the Son of God with "I am" sayings only after Peter's confession (a bit more than half way through the six-hour film).[2] These sayings directly identify Jesus as God's Son, indeed as God on earth in John.

By reserving the "I am" sayings until after Peter's confession, *Jesus of Nazareth* smoothly merges John's perspective with that of the other three Gospels. It makes historically sensible Jesus' self-characterization and self-understanding in all four Gospels. Gospel inconsistency has been deftly explained. Unlike the Jesus of *The Greatest Story Ever Told*, who is openly the descendent Logos of God, the Jesus of *Jesus of Nazareth* becomes dramatically more interesting as his self-revelation develops.

The film's appearance of completeness belies significant omissions of canonical Gospel material. The following noteworthy episodes are absent: temptation, wedding at Cana, transfiguration, stilling of the storm, walking on the water, and encounters with lepers. Added to the Gospel material is significant legendary and fictional material with regard to the family of Jesus. In addition, the film develops a thoroughly fictitious theory of the betrayal by Judas and appears to inherit the previous traditions of the Cinematic Savior that show a tendency to de-emphasize the miracles of Jesus that violate natural law. By deleting the temptation scene, no place is made in the movie for an examination of Jesus' conflict with himself, or with Satan. In addition it has put on screen for the first time for an American audience a decidedly Catholic telling of the family life of Jesus. Judas continues to be of great importance and is elevated into a misunderstood, tragic character who doesn't really betray. Jesus himself becomes a religious reformer of Judaism while also showing himself as the divine founder of Christianity. In this context, the sufferings of Jesus remain muted so as to not detract from his spiritual value to the audience. In this last, *Jesus of Nazareth* follows the earlier films.

JESUS THE JEW

The audience sees the adult Jesus (Robert Powell) for the first time through the eyes of John the Baptist (Michael York) approximately 1:39

into the film. The scene recalls a similar technique used in *King of Kings* (1927) where Jesus first appears through the healed eyes of a blind child. Jesus himself has become younger, but the concentration of the camera on his stare remains consistent with previous Jesus movies. While a dove appears, John recites, "This is my beloved son" from a New Testament not yet written. Here and elsewhere *Jesus of Nazareth* naturalizes the miraculous in keeping with a modern, yet faith-based perspective. He is the Jewish son of Mary and Joseph who fulfills all righteousness.

This film, more than any other, presents Jesus as a product of Jewish piety and culture. *Jesus of Nazareth* takes time to develop a variety of groups and sects within Judaism. Small village, family, and synagogue-centered Judaism gives birth to and nurtures the young Jesus. A large part of the opening of the film introduces us to Joseph, Mary, and her mother Anna. Much of the material is not found in the Gospels. Some is based on later legend. Some is creative fiction. While we view a representation of Jewish life that has great verisimilitude, the integration of old traditional Christian stories and visual motifs ensures that the film culture remains familiar to the intended audience.

Jesus of Nazareth engages in the strongest free fictionalization of characters in the prebirth stories about Jesus. Joseph, particularly, is a pious man who loves children, teaching them in his workshop. Mary (Olivia Hussey, who previously played in Zeffirelli's *Romeo and Juliet*) is devout and faithful. She is the most beautiful Mother of Jesus to be portrayed on screen. Her scene with Elizabeth provides an enactment of adoration equal to that of later church piety. Far from there being a scandal at her pregnancy, the local rabbi acts as a compassionate voice, encouraging Joseph's faith. The betrothal and marriage scenes occur almost as "Kodak" moments where the viewer is included in the wedding album.[3] These ancient Jews act like typical suburban Americans.

The villagers possess sophisticated theology and keen political insight. Every action seems grounded in prophecy. *Jesus of Nazareth* effectively moves prophetic/biblical quotation from voice-over, as in *The Greatest Story Ever Told*, to speeches by subsidiary characters. One has the sense that this is what DeMille was attempting with his composite titles in *King of Kings* (1927), but the limitations of silent film prevented a full integration of biblical quotation into a naturalistic story. The technique enhances the credibility of the story and establishes the faith of specific characters who stand in for the viewers. The viewer is a person of faith who would have believed had he or she been there. While the Gospel of Matthew, for example, contains 17 direct citations of the prophets and another five recognizable quotations, prophetic texts in *Jesus of Nazareth* become an occasion for monologues of faith by significant characters.

Jesus' hometown anticipates a messiah who will come according to scripture and lead them into full righteousness, thereby delivering them from the tyranny of Herod and the Romans. Their faith will be betrayed by the religious leadership and political machinations in the city of Jerusalem.

Jesus himself is born according to the prophets. He is without doubt Jewish, circumcised on the eighth day, bar-mitzvahed at 12. He impresses all by his wisdom. When he appears as an adult, his acts of righteousness emerge flawlessly from his childhood experiences.

Nevertheless, the representation of Jesus introduces decidedly non-Jewish elements. Jesus himself becomes physically transformed. The dark-eyed, dark-haired infant miraculously becomes an angelic preteen, blue-eyed and blond. His adult depiction retains the penetrating blue eyes of Hollywood tradition. The Jewishness of Jesus assured by dialogue and plot plays against the visual representation of a thoroughly Anglo Cinematic Savior.

Throughout the film Jesus acts as a master of scripture, a healer, and above all else a teacher and reconciler of men. The most vivid scene occurs at the house of Matthew the tax collector, where Jesus, through artful storytelling, illustrates that the "heart of the law is mercy." Jesus, Son of God, reconciles man to man, represented by Peter and Matthew. His response to occupation and grinding taxation (without representation) is to teach a minor morality. Peter becomes the example for this conversion, "I am just a stupid man . . . forgive me, Master." The scene by its duration (10 minutes) gives the viewer a real-time appreciation of Jesus as he must have taught.

Jesus, the Messiah, Son of God, answers the longing in Judaism for a "law alive in our hearts" as John, the disciple, says. While Jesus is shown as the master of scripture, then as healer and parable teller, there remains a sense in the series that Jesus grows steadily into his full divinity until at the confession of Peter he becomes "I am"—the fully realized Son of God. In this calm state of self-possession, and with this simple, absolute statement of existence, he ultimately goes to his death. There are no surprises from this Jesus. *Jesus of Nazareth* portrays a fully realized, harmonious view of a Jesus whose actions and character make perfect sense to a believing audience.

JUDAS

The Hollywood representation of Judas had already left behind that of the Gospels prior to *Jesus of Nazareth*. Judas entered the tradition in

King of Kings (1927) as a social climber who wanted to ride Jesus' popularity to political power. *King of Kings* (1961) developed Judas as a zealot who had to choose the way of peace or the way of war, and who falls by refusing faith in peace. *The Greatest Story Ever Told* depicted Judas as a confused man who ultimately functioned as a symbolic final sacrifice to the old religion of Judaism. *Jesus Christ Superstar* elevated him to the level of tragic hero/anti-hero undone by his own moralism, but who is rewarded by a beatific vision of heaven. The Cinematic Savior thus seems to require an equally interesting character opposite him. In no movie does Peter fit the bill. Instead Judas becomes the focus of the modern audience's attention, and he achieves that role in a manner totally foreign to the Gospels.

Jesus of Nazareth contributes to the development of the tradition of Judas. In this film his faith is genuine, but he is duped. In order to accomplish this particular renovation of Judas, the master political animal, Zerah, must be created. We met his predecessor in *The Greatest Story Ever Told* in the character of Sorek, but here, in a script written by Anthony Burgess of *A Clockwork Orange* fame and enhanced by Zeffirelli's direction, Zerah functions as the true villain. Judas becomes one of us in *Jesus of Nazareth*. He is humanized and fallible, and so we can identify with him in a way that we cannot with Jesus. Unlike the ancient world that accepted that a human could simply be bad or a servant of evil, the modern audience requires an explanation of the bad man's motives.

Jesus of Nazareth uses the Judas–Zerah subplot as a means of muting or nearly eliminating the potential for an anti-Jewish reading of the story of Jesus. The solution to the theological and historical conundrum of how a disciple could actually betray his divine master is made compelling by the film's artistry. In this case, the dramatic verisimilitude coincides with modern attitudes so closely that its very seamlessness, its full explanatory value, should make us pause. When we are comfortable with a representation, particularly of another historical period or culture, it may be that we are seeing what we want to see, not what is. As we shall see, the fascination with Judas continues in *The Last Temptation of Christ* and *The Passion of the Christ*. As much as Jesus, Judas gives us clues to shifts in the popular American religious imagination and theology.

Jesus of Nazareth presents Judas in sharp contrast to Peter, who is depicted as a plain and not very sophisticated fisherman. Judas makes his living as a scribe and translator in a "country of many languages." He truly believes in Jesus as a priest-king Messiah who will unify the religious and the political elements in Israel. In the scene of Peter's confession, Judas therefore presses Jesus to go to Jerusalem. Judas does not understand Jesus' prediction of the Passion. Therefore, Judas's lack of understanding becomes the avenue for Zerah's machinations. Ultimately, Jesus will admit to di-theism, that is, he will claim to be God alongside God.

Judas's mistake is to see Jesus as a traditional Jewish Messiah who is both king and high priest. He cannot understand Jesus' break with external religion and move to concentrate on the internal transformation of humans. In the film Jesus unifies his roles as teacher, miracle worker, and prophet in his reality as the Son of God, who shows Israel rebirth from within. When Judas agrees with Zerah to deliver Jesus it is not, for him or for Jesus, a betrayal, but an opportunity for Jesus to show himself as the Messiah who is king and high priest, his true self, Judas thinks. Judas simply believes in the wrong outcome. Zerah pays him, but money was never Judas's motive. In grief at his mistake, not at a premeditated sin, Judas hangs himself with the money belt. The motif was introduced by *Jesus Christ Superstar* and repeats itself to different effect in *The Passion of the Christ*.

What Jesus makes apparent in the Supper scene is his death as suffering servant. *Jesus of Nazareth* couples this largely Jewish motif, derived from Isaiah, with the depiction of Jesus as Son of God in its Johannine interpretation. He is truly God. Jesus' salvation supersedes that of Judaism and its political-religious hierarchy found in the temple and Sanhedrin. As Jesus himself admits before the high priest, "I am." Judas believes in Jesus as a good Jew, coupling his messiahship with Jewish institutions. Thus, he is the tragic Jew, but not a Christian.

In Judas's stead, Zerah acts as the betrayer. He sets up Jesus' condemnation before the Sanhedrin. *Jesus of Nazareth* constructs a hearing, not a trial, before the Sanhedrin. The real trial is secular and occurs later before Pilate. The Sanhedrin appears as a rather contentious theological debating society. For Caiaphas it is a theological problem: Is Jesus a blasphemer? It is also a political problem: Jesus jeopardizes the whole nation.

The scene before the Sanhedrin completes the contrast established throughout the film between town and city. According to the film, early Christians are drawn from solid, small-town, common stock. The intellectuals and national leadership are largely relegated to the old religion, with the notable exceptions of Nicodemus and Joseph of Arimathea. They constitute a persuadable middle ground of legal, prophetic interpretation. *Jesus of Nazareth* thereby deftly finesses the old problem of anti-Semitism while preserving Christian successionism. Judaism has been left behind.

The clear preference for pious small-town Judaism to the elites of the city means that the religious ceremonies are largely limited to those of the synagogue and not of the temple. Judaism as a sacrificial religion remains virtually absent. Thereby, the American audience's religious practices, being largely congregational and democratic, look and feel like the practices of small-town Judaism as shown on screen. Jesus is a generic salt-of-the-earth American whose natural appeal is to piety, sanctity, and simplicity. Judas becomes a scholar, misled by an astute and elite politician, while the religious leadership quibbles.

HOLLYWOOD'S MAKING OF THE AMERICAN CHRIST

While *Jesus of Nazareth* was initially a joint British-Italian production, American TV audiences adopted its view of Jesus wholeheartedly. Zeffirelli had two controlling ideas: The Gospel of John was an eye-witness account of the life of Jesus; and Jesus should be presented as thoroughly Jewish.[4] Zeffirelli had already shown his mastery of the film medium, and his style very much appealed to Americans in *Romeo and Juliet* (1968) and in *Brother Sun, Sister Moon* (1973). With *Jesus of Nazareth*, he creates the miniseries and remains its most accomplished director.

The television screen, which dwells within the space of the family, allows for an intimacy not available on the large screen. *Jesus of Nazareth* is distinctly not spectacle; it is postcards from the life of Christ. Zeffirelli paints his scenes with light, evoking but not copying church masters. The Supper reminds us of da Vinci's, but it is not an imitation.

Fifty percent of U.S. television viewers watched the series' first showing of two three-hour segments on Palm Sunday and Easter on NBC in 1977.[5] *Jesus of Nazareth* almost overnight became the epitome of the Cinematic Savior. Like DeMille, Ray, and Stevens before him and Scorsese and Gibson after, Zeffirelli saw his work as an expression of his own faith. He even produced a book, *Il mio Gesu* (My Jesus), in which he discusses his work. As Baugh illustrates, the book had a direct effect on the interpretation of the series.[6]

In casting, Zeffirelli used a who's who of international actors. Who can forget Sir Lawrence Olivier as Nicodemus at the foot of the cross? The casting of Robert Powell moves to a younger, but no less ethereal Jesus than Max von Sydow or H. B. Warner, and avoids the youth of Jeffrey Hunter and the anti-heroic physique and voice of Ted Neely. We now have a Jesus who walks off the pages of Sunday school quarterlies and into historic verisimilitude and intimacy. As never before, Jesus is Jewish and our familiar Christian savior.

The palette of the film is warm but never lurid—intimate and neutral. The sacramental view becomes the camera view and does not appear foreign or excessive. *The Last Temptation of Christ* and *The Passion of the Christ* can then assume this as the basis for their effect by introducing a decidedly more lurid palette that later passes for realism.

In its last two-hour segment, *Jesus of Nazareth* adopts the pace established by *King of Kings* (1927). The concentration on the Crucifixion, bracketed by the raising of Lazarus and the resurrection of Jesus, becomes an established set piece of American film. *The Passion of the Christ* owes much of its camera work to *Jesus of Nazareth*.

Jesus of Nazareth takes over and converts the Protestant mainstream tradition ended by *The Greatest Story Ever Told*. It ignores the cultural shifts presaged by *King of Kings* (1961) and hammered at in *Jesus Christ Superstar*. The 60s did not happen as far as *Jesus of Nazareth* is concerned. What we have is a decided infusion of Catholic iconic vigor that is acceptable to the Evangelical church movement.

Jesus of Nazareth produces an absolutely believable perspective for believers. The camera eye is always the unblinking eye of human belief. God, we assume, is present, though never directly invoked by means of the high shot. We never have God's perspective, or for that matter Jesus'. No God shots at the baptism, no high shot from the cross. The camera creates and even acts as viewer who believes throughout. The power of the camera is the power to establish seamless truth. This makes the film's theology all the more effective.

THE CANONICAL THEOLOGY

Jesus of Nazareth depends for its authenticity on a careful weaving together of biblical references in the last four hours after the traditional legends appear in hours one and two. This biblical reference is reinforced by a carefully drawn tableau of Jewish society in Palestine that remains familiar enough to be a comfortable, detailed setting for the American religious imagination. It contains no original nor offensive theory or insight into Jewish-Roman relations. It remains captivated by the same view enunciated originally in *King of Kings* (1927). The Jews were oppressed by the Romans but more particularly by their own hierarchy.

It accomplishes a view that appeals particularly to an emergent Evangelical *and* Catholic religious mainstream, constructing an easily digestible theology for the church-attending believer. Hence, it accumulates a seamless mythic field for late twentieth-century and early twenty-first-century Hollywood filmmakers and their audiences. Its timelessness is guaranteed because Jesus is the Son of God, the suffering servant who represents a proper inward morality. Jesus saves us from our sorrows and afflictions, not from supernatural evil or even sin. He founds a Christianity, as predicted by the prophets, that will supersede the old religion of Judaism.

The authenticity of *Jesus of Nazareth* is really the accumulated authenticity of the Hollywood tradition developed in *King of Kings* (1927), *King of Kings* (1961), and *The Greatest Story Ever Told*, now displayed on the family television set owned by both Catholics and Protestants. For the first time in the history of the Cinematic Jesus, the traditional barriers that relegated Catholic sensibilities to European-produced films, for example, *Il vangelo Matteo* (1966), are removed, and Catholic piety becomes as mainstream as Wheaties. I suspect that even before *Jesus of Nazareth*, perhaps even with DeMille's *King of Kings*, the movie-going and, finally, television-watching public failed to make close comparison to either biblical record or the even more arcane historical reconstructions of scholars. Instead they responded to each new representation of the Cinematic Savior according to their own religious and theological set of values, a set that is over time increasingly determined by movies and television. This is not a theology of the seminary or church, but of a living room steadily defined by media. Therefore, it does little good to critique a Jesus film as inauthentic when authenticity is only measurable with respect to the media and the film tradition. *Jesus of Nazareth* is the repository of authentic Hollywood tradition.

The theology of *Jesus of Nazareth* includes an artistic handling of the problem of Christian anti-Semitism. By constructing an exceptionally plausible theory of how Jesus might have been betrayed and put to death, the film shows how the Gospel writers, even the 11 disciples themselves, could be mistaken. Here the death did not happen as the Gospels show, because their writers could never have known of the machinations of Zerah and the duping of Judas. Left intact, however, is the clear displacement of Judaism by Christianity in accordance with God's presumed will. This element is driven home to the believing audience by characters played by accomplished actors who interpret the life through the assured speech of the prophets.

In the New Testament, most notably in the Gospel of Matthew, the prophets are used to interpret the life of Jesus. When a reader, a faithful reader, reads the text, that reader sees those words as retrospectively spoken by a fellow Christian, however anachronistic that may rationally be. The brilliance of *Jesus of Nazareth* is to place this idea of prophetic fulfillment into the mouths of those watching Jesus during his life. We are placed in the life story and hear his actions interpreted by other Jews. The sense is that the full Christian faith is now being displayed for us as Jesus' fellow Jews experienced him. We are able to watch Jesus and decide for ourselves about him first hand. According to *Jesus of Nazareth*, Jesus' life and death save. Resurrection is only a sign of God's approval.

The Jews in the series are divided into believers and unbelievers. Jesus, however, is so obviously the fulfillment of Israel's hopes that one unintended risk of the film is to hold the unbelievers responsible for the spiritual blindness that is perhaps more reprehensible, because more personal, than a simple political mistake. All unbelievers, but especially Jewish unbelievers, fall as Judas falls. While the series was the best received of the Cinematic Saviors by the American Jewish community, it may in reality be the most dangerous, because here history becomes absolutely indistinguishable from myth. The Jews really do have no excuse, except their own hardness of heart.

The theology attached to this powerful engine of representation, however, is in no way unusual or challenging. Jesus' character has been assimilated to a vast undisputed middle ground of Christian middle-class sensibilities. He is not about political or social action. There are few representations of the truly poor or outcasts. If Jesus speaks of the "poor" we understand he speaks of the spiritually poor, like us. The key scenes with Zerah, Judas, and Jesus almost directly deny any social implications of Jesus' message. Change is a change of heart. Thus, Peter may become a friend of Matthew the tax collector.

The theological climax of the film comes at the Crucifixion. Nicodemus clearly identifies Jesus as the suffering servant through a prolonged monologue derived selectively from Isaiah 53.[7] The scene also personalizes the individual experiences of main characters including the Mother, Magdalene, Martha, the centurion, and John the disciple. Close-ups of each portray this moment as the acme of grief as well as of inner transformation. The drama and pain of Crucifixion is subdued. This allows the audience a slow contemplation without the distraction of lurid sadism. The flogging/scourging that precedes it is brutal but does not overly emphasize derision or sadism. Jesus himself is not involved in a superhuman struggle against evil, pain, or death. There is hardly a trace of self-doubt; rather the story is told for the onlooker. Salvation comes through a dramatic, inward struggle with suffering, or as Nicodemus adds to the words of Isaiah, "Through his stripes we are healed . . . and *Born Again*." Thus the quintessential scholarly Jew pronounces the beginning of Christian theology.

Jesus of Nazareth, as *Ben-Hur*, presents the rain that follows the death of Jesus not as judgment but as mercy. Peter, lying in a doorway, evokes the pain of betrayal and delivers a cry for personal help. Later in the upper room he will lay the blame on the disciples: The Sanhedrin did not know him, we did and deserted. Jesus, appearing, forgives all.

Jesus of Nazareth here continues to solve the problem of anti-Semitism by distributing the guilt for Jesus' death to all. *Jesus of Nazareth* expresses a comfort with the miraculous intervention of God in its depiction of the raising of the Daughter of Jairus, the raising of Lazarus, and, most telling, the Resurrection of Jesus. All is done naturally and without much fanfare. What we see here is the new assumption in Jesus films, that divine power easily, naturally emerges where needed. Hereafter this sacramental view may be assumed for film, although from time to time we will notice a modern discomfort break through in even the most sacramental of films. In such a perspective the modern has been displaced by the assumption of some sort of supernatural order always available for film representation.

Jesus of Nazareth removes any real suggestion of the apocalypse from Jesus' preaching or life. It emphasizes an inner transformation of individuals to a life of true morality. The inner conversion comes about by contemplation of his death, which heals. Jesus dies as a martyr to human suffering. His advocacy of the poor and his fellowship with sinners does not really lead to his death. This Cinematic Savior succeeds in representing the personal frustrations of the pious of America through their televisions. In the rendition of the Cinematic Savior in *Jesus of Nazareth*, the identification of the American suburbanite with the ancient peasant, shopkeeper, and small-town carpenter provides the avenue through which theology passes from the Savior to the viewer.

Even though the economic reality of 1970s America included a large and fairly affluent middle class, we continued to see ourselves nostalgically as small farmers and townspeople. In this way we kept to our theological moorings. While in *King of Kings* (1927) the move was toward an industrialized, modern city, the move in *Jesus of Nazareth* is towards the suburbs. Not until the popular work of Steven Spielberg does Hollywood produce a specific suburban American iconography that qualifies as myth. His work emerges, tellingly, from a stable set of motifs developed first in television by such characters as Rob and Laura Petrie and Lucy and Ricky Ricardo. Similarly, *Jesus of Nazareth* stabilizes a full-blown iconography that includes a large set of solid characters that can then be sampled by later Jesus films.

Insofar as it was Zeffirelli's intention to make a didactic film for a mass audience at what he perceived as a moment of moral crisis, his film succeeds.[8] Arguably, *Jesus of Nazareth* remains unsurpassed in the size of its viewing audience and in its later influence among films about Jesus and upon our consciousness as well. It establishes in the media a new, fifth gospel, which "transforms the prophetic biblical content and themes into popular spectacle, that brings favorable reaction from which one critic calls 'the mass of believers-consumers.'"[9] This transformation of the Gospels into a commodity that targets a new subset of consumers underlies the tendency of Hollywood's approach to Jesus. Even other film genres that appeal to the Jesus story will be influenced by *Jesus of Nazareth*.

This American Christ collects the common American experience of Jesus. He no longer must be seen as an exclusively Protestant or Catholic possession. Nor is he, strictly speaking, relegated to the space of sacredness. He belongs to the faithful American Christian consumer. The Cinematic Savior now expresses a new and significant Christian mainstream divorced from a history of ethnic tensions and amalgamated into a common American mythology. If there are differences between groups of the faithful, they are sufficiently glossed over so that even, "Those representing evangelical Christianity operating out of a framework of biblical inerrancy and emphasizing personal salvation, generally liked the film as a Christian statement."[10] Somehow this group can ignore or set aside the highly Catholic elements of the film for the sake of a Christian statement perceived as standing over and against the secularities of unbelievers. *Jesus of Nazareth* culls its audience from the faithful. And this new mainstream exercises a powerful effect on the future of Jesus in film.

6

THE LAST TEMPTATION OF CHRIST:
THE PSYCHOLOGICAL PROBLEM
OF GOD IN A BODY

THE TRIANGLE REDIRECTED

The plot of *The Last Temptation of Christ* hangs on the interaction of Magdalene with Jesus and of Judas with Jesus. Magdalene and Judas never interact on screen. Thus Jesus appears driven forward by them both. He seems constantly torn between their desires. We have a reconfiguring of the triangle first constructed in *King of Kings* (1927) but to an entirely different effect.

Christianity, both in its official theologies and popular conceptions, has never come to terms with the mystery of the mythological duality of the incarnation of God in Jesus Christ: Jesus is both God and Man. The Gospels, canonical and noncanonical, themselves depict the problem in poetic terms, seldom dogmatically (for example, John 1:1–19). On its face, from the first frame Martin Scorsese sets out to explore this mystery. *The Last Temptation of Christ* further develops the tradition of directly investigating the Christ as an anti-hero of spiritual self-exploration begun by *Jesus Christ Superstar*. It appeals to images of Jesus taken directly from the history of Hollywood's Cinematic Savior. And, it retains the emphasis on sex, melodrama, and sadism begun by *King of Kings* (1927). This, more than its relatively orthodox resolution of the problem of "God in a bod," marks it as part of the Hollywood mainstream. Retrospectively, it now appears much more conventional than it did when it was released.

At that time, the movie was preemptively condemned, picketed, and almost forced to the shelf before release. Its postmodern incorporation of traditional Hollywood representations in a new, more sacramental cinematography is marked by the relentless inversion of almost every traditional and modern expectation of Jesus. This gives it its fresh and challenging perspective. Its plot, characterization, and structure invite a loose and associative (rather than simply linear) understanding of the story of Jesus, which makes it difficult for the audience to understand. The film, while flawed, gives us an opportunity to understand America's struggle with its own Savior and, through him, itself.

Many reviewers, and most audiences, I suspect, try to view *The Last Temptation of Christ* as a simple narrative film, which is to say the film presumes its viewers accept for the duration of the film that these events happened. At times Scorsese almost studiously reshoots standard scenes used from DeMille to Zeffirelli, but he does so to undo their effect. Because of his undoing, his inversions, those who assume that this is a simple narrative film become confused by a variety of techniques, including an internal voice-over narrative by Jesus himself, a staged nonrealistic mise-en-scene, and a contemporary musical score (the score, by Peter Gabriel, perfects the style begun by *Jesus Christ Superstar*). These changes undermine the viewer's faith in the reality that the camera presents.

With *The Last Temptation of Christ*, the postmodern condition and Christian theology combine in the Hollywood mainstream. By "postmodern condition" I mean not a philosophical school, or an avant-garde film style, but rather the situation that comes about as America leaves behind the consensus that governed the modern period and begins to reassemble the fragments of its previous ideology. The film is filled with doubt and search, as is America. Scorsese's strength in this film lies in his attempt to reassemble some of America's mythology visually.

In the opening scene, Jesus lies in an olive garden. A high shot establishes an apparently omniscient point of view. The traditional Hollywood convention dictates to the audience that God is watching. We even witness the trees unnaturally rustled by an unseen presence. But this perspective immediately comes into question. Jesus' own inner voice narrates the scene. Moreover, Jesus' self-consciousness is tortured and unsure. Through him the film posits that the entire story that we are about to see is Jesus' own psychological search. We watch the remainder of the film as his experience of his own struggle. Because he finally submits to Crucifixion, is this perspective his from the cross, or even after?

Since the dualities of spirit and body, male and female, celibacy and sexuality recur in dialogue and visual representation in the film, an association develops that God is the force driving Jesus to choose the first of each pair and reject the second. But, as Mary the mother puts it early on, it could be the Devil. To which Jesus responds "What if it is God?" The film dramatically builds toward Jesus' choice to deny the body represented by the desire for a woman and family and thereby to save humanity.

In the final scene Jesus' vision from the cross shows his decision. Jesus on his deathbed 40 years after leaving the cross, surrounded by his family, is visited by his disciples. They come from the siege of Jerusalem by the Romans. Last to arrive is Judas. True to his character throughout the film, he comes with blood on his hands from the struggle, and he brings direct revelation. Unlike the Judas of *Jesus Christ Superstar* he knows what must take place, "What is good for a man isn't good for God. . . . No sacrifice . . . no salvation." Jesus has experienced his doubts and now chooses to crawl back to the cross. On the way he confesses, "I am a selfish unfaithful son. I want to bring salvation . . . to be crucified and rise again." With his final words, "It is finished," bells, drums, and a visual explosion of red light occur.

This last filmic light phenomenon references the "Star Gate" sequence of *2001: A Space Odyssey* (Stanley Kubrick, 1968). In that movie, however, a final rebirth of the Star Child indicates a distribution or evolution of the human onto the backdrop of the universe, quite literally and visually. Here, no concluding Resurrection scene validates for us Jesus' choice. Individual audience members must decide for themselves whether or not salvation has come through this sacrifice.

THE RELATIONSHIP OF JUDAS TO JESUS

In *The Last Temptation of Christ* Judas completes the American movie trajectory established for him by previous films. Steadily his character has been explored, brought to the fore, in an attempt to make sense of his betrayal. While *Jesus Christ Superstar* brought Judas back from heaven, in *The Last Temptation of Christ* he is the hero from his opening scenes.

Judas appears on screen almost immediately after Jesus' opening struggle in the garden, slapping Jesus around for collaborating with the Romans and serving as their crossmaker. Judas himself is a revolutionary and terrorist, set on violence to purge Israel of Roman occupation. While Judas literally struggles with the Romans in the subsequent scene, physically breaking one's neck, Jesus struggles with the voices in his head.

In the subsequent appearances of Judas, Jesus manages to convince Judas that he, Jesus, is being led by God, who "will do the talking." Judas promises to be the enforcer. Deviation from the path by Jesus means death at Judas's hands. This early scene prefigures the final role that Judas will play as designated aid, not betrayer.

Throughout the film Judas is the major theological interlocutor who eclipses all of the other disciples in screen time and therefore also in his dramatic interaction with Jesus. The film reinforces this role again and again so that the movie takes on aspects of the Hollywood "buddy" movie with two male friends aiding each other in a joint quest.

While Magdalene will be used as the principle symbol of the major duel between flesh and spirit (as being a duel between woman and man) Judas's contribution to this same duality is to interpret the body as the means to social action. For Jesus the spirit comes first, and internal change as the conversion of the soul of man is his priority. For Judas the foundation is the body, by which he means revolutionary action. Jesus wishes initially to break the chain of evil with love. These two characters present for audience consideration the almost classic problem in American religious thought: Does the kingdom of God, or in the theological terms of the film, the world of God, enter by internal purification of the spirit, or through social action and reform?

Judas states the classic social gospel; Jesus, on the other hand, the inward piety that leads to a new evolved spirituality. For Jesus society is not the problem; from his spiritual perspective, the ills of society will be overcome by an inward journey to God. Therefore, the film will highlight, through Jesus, the theology of inward change. Because of this, the film comments little or not at all on issues of social justice, poverty, and riches, issues that can be found in the preaching of the Jesus of the canonical Gospels. The barren landscape of Galilee and Judea in the film comes to represent the harsh and tortured existence of Jesus' soul and ours. Satan here is not, as in *The Greatest Story Ever Told*, a spokesperson for the easy life of luxury, but rather the one who tempts Jesus to a simple home life.

Judas's own belief in and devotion to Jesus never wavers. In the key scene after Jesus returns from the desert to displace the gospel of love with the gospel of the axe, a war on evil, Judas is the first to fall to his knees and proclaim Jesus as *Adonai,* (the Hebrew word for Lord used in pious circles as a substitute for the holy the name of God), after witnessing the bleeding heart of Jesus.

The scene is filled with allusions to traditional stories. Judas scornfully and ironically designates Peter as a rock, whose mind cannot be changed. The strongest inversion is Jesus ripping out his heart, a traditional symbol of his compassion, as a metaphor for the war on Satan. God, Jesus says, is inside of us. We make war on the Devil by healing the sick, attacking the rich, and even the temple. For the moment, Jesus becomes the revolutionary Judas wants. The casting out and curing are the process of his perfection.

This perfecting, shot in clear homage to the healing sequence in *Jesus Christ Superstar*, shows Judas supporting an exhausted Jesus. Arrival in the temple and its cleansing come to naught as Jesus fails to lead a rebellion and instead, with the stigmata of Crucifixion miraculously displayed, he flees with the support of Judas to change his mission yet again.

As in *Jesus of Nazareth* previously and *The Passion of the Christ* subsequently, Isaiah 53 becomes the controlling theology for interpreting Jesus' Crucifixion. Here Jesus tells Judas that Isaiah visited him in a dream and opened the scroll to him. The viewer should note that in the film the scroll is actually blank. Nevertheless, Jesus reads, "He has bourne our faults, he was wounded for our transgressions yet he opened not his mouth . . . like a lamb led to slaughter." Jesus himself, however, lacks the strength or courage to see this divine vision through. Judas is the strongest; he must betray, says Jesus. The betrayal, however, is not betrayal; rather, it is a fulfillment of Jesus' mission. Therefore, Judas now has been reinterpreted to sit at the right hand of Jesus and hold him to his mission. In the film only now, confirmed by his own reading of a blank scroll, does Jesus know he must die. He also predicts his apocalyptic return. He will come back to judge. Judas is the agent, the enforcer, of the will of God when Jesus himself is too weak to fulfill his destiny alone. We are left wondering if this is a divine vision or mere hallucination.

MAGDALENE'S INFLUENCE ON JESUS

In *The Last Temptation of Christ* the character of Magdalene becomes, like Judas, even further constructed in keeping with the trajectory in earlier films. No longer, however, is she a courtesan. Nor is she simply the adulteress, nor a small-time village harlot. Here she embraces the life of a full-blown prostitute out of an apparent disappointed romance with Jesus. She so dominates the structure of the film that her major scenes bracket the beginning and end of Jesus' temptations. In this way her individuality becomes subsumed under a larger symbol. Or, as the devil in the garb of a prepubescent guardian angel says, "All women are the same; there is only one woman."

Her symbol is the snake. The symbol is fundamental to the concept of temptation, since it refers to the story of the Adam and Eve. In two of Jesus' visions Magdalene is the voice of the snake, offering Jesus her body and children. Similarly in the scene with Jesus in the brothel she tempts him with her body, "Here is my body; save it," an inversion of the meaning of Jesus' own words in the Synoptic Gospels at the Last Supper. When he refuses, she excoriates him for his lack of manhood. He has driven her to the life of prostitution, and finally in yet another inversion she will not allow him to look at her nakedness.

The scene establishes motivation for Magdalene that explores the drama of human disappointment; it also displays Jesus as a weak, tempted, voyeuristic man, beset by his own internal conflicts. The connection of woman to fertility, visually explored in a much gentler manner in *Jesus Christ Superstar*, has now been established as the most shocking and dominating temptation for Jesus. It refers to human generation in contrast to the later spiritual generation of Jesus.

Magdalene also is absorbed into the story of the woman whom Jesus saves from stoning. The scene moves seamlessly into a halting rendition of the Sermon on the Mount, set here among the ruins of a once great civilization. Or is Palestine to be interpreted as the internal terra incognita of Jesus' tortured soul?

Even here, though Judas and Magdalene appear in the same film sequence here, they never interact dramatically. They only interact through Jesus, who shows compassion toward Magdalene in the face of Judas's accusations. Thus Magdalene, unlike Judas, remains a symbol of the Woman in this film. Unlike her use in *King of Kings* (1927) her story is not one of conversion, although after this scene she is covered and wrapped, but she remains outside the circle of the faithful, as temptation. The disciples, on the other hand, are an all-male club. Women are only there as the Woman to tempt one away from the true mission, spiritual self-realization.

In the final temptation sequence, Jesus envisions himself as walking from the cross and into marriage with Magdalene. He has sex with Magdalene while the guardian angel looks on (a very creepy bit of voyeurism that should key any viewer to the insight that this child-angel is really the Devil in disguise). For those who wish to compare the movie to the original novel, Nikos Katzanakis's depiction of the sex between Jesus and Magdalene is if anything more graphic than what takes place before us here. She and the unborn baby subsequently die.

Fertility with the beloved cannot be blessed. Magdalene as the symbol of temptation, of bodily happiness and existence reduced to sexual pleasure and family life, can easily be replaced by Mary and then her sister Martha in Jesus' temptation, in what effectively amounts to a domestication of the femme fatale. So this final vision places Jesus' final temptation clearly before the audience. The film by its iconography and emphasis has reduced the temptations of Jesus, and by its argument all men, to the temptation of Woman who represents the body, apparently whether in the brothel or the kitchen. Salvation then, on this reading, appears to come through rejection of the Woman who is an equivalent symbol to the body. The spirit is male.

This straightforward reading of the main structure of the film around the three main characters, however, demands further exploration of subsidiary themes and finally an examination of the director's style if we are to appreciate the inconclusiveness of the film's theology and iconography.

THE PSYCHOLOGY OF JESUS

It has become apparent that both Judas and Magdalene represent the body. Judas is the body politic of messianic action that brings about the destruction of the political forces of evil. Judas follows Jesus most closely and supports him in the final, abortive march on Jerusalem and rebellion against Rome. Even in the final temptation vision, Judas appears at the bedside, stained with blood from fighting at the siege of Jerusalem. Judas, like Barabbas in *King of Kings* (1961), refers to full-bodied political engagement. To the extent that he is the proto-Christian in the film, he may be seen to represent the path of a socially active, even revolutionary Christianity: the route to a greater or lesser extent advocated by social gospel and liberation theologies of the twentieth century.

No less than Judas, Magdalene refers to the body as the sexual, fertile, and (in the late twentieth century with its AIDS crisis) diseased body. The reduction of all sin to Woman's sin is almost, but not fully, realized by *The Last Temptation of Christ*. Here the film's theology is most like *King of Kings* (1927) where Magdalene was shown to be possessed by all seven deadly sins, thereby graphically showing the woman to be the source and repository of all vice. In *The Last Temptation of Christ* she is constructed as the dark daughter of Eve; the continuation of the Christian interpretation of the Garden of Eden, which links the sin of Eve in the eating of the tree of knowledge of good and evil to the fall of all mankind.

The ties become apparent in Jesus' own temptation in the desert, which follows immediately upon his leaving Magdalene's brothel. Jesus draws a circle and meditates. A snake with Magdalene's voice tempts him to family, woman, bed, and breasts. The direct tie to Eden could not be clearer. A lion then appears, tempting him to world domination. The voice belongs to Judas. The lion refers to the biblical symbol of the House of David, the original Messiah of Israel. Finally, a spout of fire appears. Initially the association within film tradition and biblical tradition goes to the God of Israel. *The Ten Commandments* (Cecil B. DeMille, 1956) repeatedly uses fire imagery to refer to God, as does the Book of Exodus. But, as with so many other traditional images, *The Last*

Temptation of Christ inverts the reference, and along with the audience, Jesus sees the fire as Satan himself. Within the circle, now a circle of temptation, an apple tree appears. The popular, though non-Biblical, reference is to the tree of knowledge in the Garden of Eden. The Book of Genesis nowhere designates the tree as an apple tree. Jesus tastes the fruit, filled with blood, and concludes that it is time for the message of the axe. As the subsequent events make clear, this too is a temptation sent by Satan.

The Last Temptation of Christ remains consistent from the first scene onward. The temptations of Jesus are inside his head. They are the psychic projections of his tortured consciousness. The temptations are double-layered. First, it is clear that the choice is between the Spirit and the Flesh. And the flesh includes not only woman, family, bed, and breasts, but political power as well. *The Last Temptation of Christ*, unlike Christian tradition and previous Hollywood films, offers us a Jesus who struggles psychologically.

To effect this psychological struggle, Jesus becomes in *The Last Temptation of Christ* a weak, vacillating man, unsure of his mission. The only segment of film where he seems relatively self-assured is in his mission of the axe. Even here, however, his discussions with Judas reflect a weakness: Jesus requires constant encouragement. Scorsese follows the characterization under development in previous Hollywood films. He gathers up the passivity of earlier Jesuses in *King of Kings* (1927) and *The Greatest Story Ever Told*. He then aligns these images with the characterization of Jesus as anti-hero begun by *Jesus Christ Superstar*. *Jesus Christ Superstar*, however, makes Jesus' final choice to die an existential leap of faith into the arms of an unknowable God. *The Last Temptation of Christ* displays Jesus as a tortured psyche whose final decision could as well be the delusions of a dying man as the decision of a man of faith. Through the Hollywood tradition Jesus becomes progressively younger. He is cut in the mold of Hollywood's New Man. The internal voices driving Willem Dafoe in *The Last Temptation of Christ* are of a piece with those that drive Marlon Brando in *On the Waterfront* or James Dean in *Rebel without a Cause*. The New Man has now been baptized into the story of the American Christ.

WHAT TO MAKE OF JOHN THE BAPTIST, LAZARUS, SAUL?

The subsidiary characters of John the Baptist, Lazarus, and Saul offer a perpetual assault of inversions. The baptism by John appears after Jesus' retreat to the desert monastery, after he gathers disciples, and just prior to his temptation in the desert. The film creates some possible confusion between John and the master of the monastery, who had, after his death, appeared miraculously to Jesus. They are played by different actors, but their visual representations make it easy to confuse the two. Thereby, John the Baptist may be seen as a reincarnation in some sense of the personality of the master. This may account for why Jesus subsequently follows John's advice to take up the axe. His own visionary experiences also seem to validate John's counsel.

The film departs markedly from previous representations of Jesus' baptism, most notably as depicted in *The Greatest Story Ever Told*. In *The Last Temptation of Christ*, we have a scene of an ecstatic, baptismal cult. The crowd is naked and gyrating. John is shown as a strange, apocalyptic prophet. Angry, he demands repentance in view of impending judgment. Jesus, obviously, submits to John's message of repentance and in his subsequent vision in the desert accepts the role of apocalyptic prophet and divine judge demanded by John. The clear submission of Jesus to John departs from previous representations that have shown Jesus' superiority and sense of divine mission as an alternative and displacement to John's theology.

More impressive is the reversal in the raising of Lazarus. In previous films, this scene has been repeated as a keynote miracle. It is enacted on screen in *King of Kings* (1927) and in *The Greatest Story Ever Told* as the final most dramatic miracle of Jesus. Especially in *The Greatest Story Ever Told* it becomes so overwhelming cinematically that it even dwarfs the Resurrection of Jesus himself.

In *The Last Temptation of Christ*, the scene depicts a genuine struggle between Jesus and death. The shot frames Jesus in the entrance to the tomb from the perspective of Lazarus himself, who reaches out and almost drags Jesus in. Its effect, however, is reversed from the traditional image by the later fate of Lazarus.

In this version, Saul assassinates Lazarus. His motivation seems to be an effort to debunk or kill the reputation of Jesus, although why Saul, here depicted as a Zealot revolutionary against Rome, wants to do so remains fuzzy. The theological dialogue between Saul and Lazarus gives the audience few if any insights into death or life. The function of the miracle in earlier films is a cathartic enactment of our own desire to find life out of the death of a loved one. The scene of the murder, while dramatic, and while it establishes the almost psychotic viciousness of Saul, serves little purpose, except perhaps to establish Saul's pre-Christian life as one zealous for some defense of his brand of Judaism.

Saul makes a further appearance within the last temptation of Jesus. As an old man Jesus meets Saul preaching his Resurrection and gaining followers for a nascent Christianity. His zealousness has been transmuted into an almost fiendish disregard for truth. Saul assures Jesus that, even if he had not been resurrected, nevertheless, he, Saul, would invent the myth of the Christ in order to give the people something to hold on to. By implication, then, Saul (Paul) becomes the founder of a false Christianity, based on a lie. As with all the scenes in Jesus' final temptation, the viewer is unsettled by the knowledge that Jesus' vision is not given by God, but by Satan. It is to that final scene, and its preparation in the Passion narrative of the film, that I now turn in order to arrive finally at some discussion of the film's attempts at mythic and theological resolutions.

HOW AND WHY DOES JESUS DIE?

Early in *The Last Temptation of Christ* we see a Roman detachment about to crucify a messianic revolutionary, with Jesus serving as crossmaker and crossbearer. Unlike previous Jesus films, the Romans in *The Last Temptation of Christ* provide a rather motley backdrop to the personal struggle of Jesus. Clearly they are the occupiers and oppressors. But we do not see the heinousness of their imperialism, or its overwhelming power. Except for their English accents (which all the evil characters—including Satan in all his guises—share), little denotes the Romans specifically. The accents follow and comment on the Hollywood convention from epic films (see especially *Spartacus*) that in some sense refers the American audience to their own experience of British imperialism during the colonial period. The point seems to be that an English accent indicates the language of evil. The film moves a Hollywood convention from an allusion to American history into the realm of the spirit.

Certainly when Pilate appears, as played by David Bowie, the surreal takes over. Pilate's tired almost burned-out delivery portrays a sense of fatigued bureaucracy and, along with the (odd) choice of having the interview in the stable (reminiscent of *Equus*), a vaguely suppressed sense of sadistic pleasure.

Ultimately, Pilate emerges as a pragamatic politician. After having heard Jesus prophesy the displacement of Rome by the World of God in terms derived from Daniel 7, Pilate reminds Jesus that there must be 3,000 skulls on Golgatha, "I do wish you people would go out and count them sometime." Rome does not want things to be changed. The scene never really enters into a genuine philosophical/theological dialogue between Jesus and Pilate. Nor does it in any way depict anything like an official hearing. For that, the most interesting scene on film really is to be found in *Jesus of Nazareth*, where Pilate (Rod Steiger) portrays both extreme fatigue at the burden of ruling an unmanageable land and a genuine theological interest in truth. Only in *Jesus of Nazareth* does Rome have a soul. Here, Romans believe nothing; they are soulless shells, possessed by evil.

The main effect of the portrayal of the Romans in *The Last Temptation of Christ* is to show them as ruthless and swift in suppressing any hint of an uprising. The film may be closer to history here than at any other point. By avoiding any real presence of official Judaism in the trial and condemnation of Jesus, *The Last Temptation of Christ* also avoids any anti-Semitism.

Like Rome, the Judaism of *The Last Temptation of Christ* provides a backdrop for Jesus' personal, inward journey. Unlike the pastiche of Rome that leaves us wondering just what connections we might make, the depiction of Judaism has a depth and an obvious referent. The Jewish world of *The Last Temptation of Christ* is really a stand-in for Catholicism. Village Judaism rejects Jesus as a crazy crank, whose asceticism has meant that his unspent semen has clouded his mind. When Jesus visits the desert assembly, what is evoked is more a monastic settlement like that of the early Christian desert fathers, but unlike that of Jewish monastics, for example, Qumran or the Theraputae. By borrowing images from Catholic monastic life and projecting them back into the time of Jesus, *The Last Temptation of Christ* shows the direct influence of the Catholic lives of the saints and medieval monasticism. Similarly, the Baptist sect, although naked and gyrating wildly, also evokes by its self-flagellation similar scenes from medieval Catholicism. There is little that is specifically Jewish in the culture from which Jesus comes, or to which he preaches. Jesus and his band are among Christians, albeit prereformation Christians.

The exception to this is found in the depiction of the Jewish temple as a blood cult. Again, the audience should not assume that the images of the Passover are historical reconstructions. The emphasis on blood sacrifice, however, adds a dimension to the cleansing that Jesus initiates in his assault on the temple. Judaism in the film is a religion of law, morality, and sacrifice, with a few ascetics on the fringes. The same might be said from the film's view point of pre-Reformation Christianity.

And so when Jesus cleanses the temple and proclaims himself the Saint of Blasphemy and states that God is an immortal spirit, not an Israelite, he proclaims himself a blasphemer against Catholic America's view of itself. Jesus points the way forward toward a "religionless" spirituality. The interpretation is a possible one: I wish the totality of the film supported such a clear interpretation. It is noteworthy that, unlike previous films, any identifiable Protestant image has disappeared. The playing field for reference in the film is now limited to images derived from the so-called secular realm and from traditional Catholicism. The Protestant modern mainstream has vanished as a live tradition for representation or reference.

The Last Temptation of Christ marks the apex of the Hollywood tradition of exonerating the Jews from responsibility for the death of Jesus, and thereby it avoids any anti-Semitic reading of Jesus' life and death. It also lacks the Christian successionism I noted in earlier films. This is understandable, since to the extent that it treats religion at all, *The Last Temptation of Christ* sees the institutions of religion generally as moribund and ineffectual. If we are to follow Christ, the inward spiritual journey is all that remains. Hence, the individual man has succeeded religions generally. Judaism falls away from consideration as a real historical force in the life of Jesus. After all, Jesus' search in *The Last Temptation of Christ* appears to be to align him with God's foreordained plan and thus his destiny. Since his message is individual, not social or institutional, then religion itself disappears.

THE CRUCIFIXION AND LAST TEMPTATION OF JESUS

The beating and scourging, while brief, is the most graphically brutal in Hollywood film to the date of its release. Many elements from this film will be reworked in *The Passion of the Christ*. Unlike *The Passion of the Christ*, however, *The Last Temptation of Christ* focuses on Jesus' human suffering. It does not offer close-ups of the soldier's pleasure at his beating. Their faces are shrouded in shadow. Jesus, and Jesus alone, stands out. The scene is brief, brutal, and matter of fact. The theology of Isaiah referenced earlier now becomes the interpretative perspective of the camera. We are shown the ways in which Jesus suffers for us. Indeed, the theological consistency from here to the cross is perhaps the most powerful single aspect of the film.

Peter denies him. The disciples run away. The crowds are variously shown to be derisive or in mourning. Musically, the score enhances horror. A judicious use of slow motion on the Via Dolorosa allows audience contemplation of the horror of the Crucifixion without directly invoking church-established piety. At Golgotha, the camera perspective moves circularly, contributing to the audience's sense that it is actually there, experiencing the scene with Jesus. It is surreal, three dimensional, and painful. Magdalene and Mary the mother are there; at one point Jesus actually apologizes for being a bad son. They both suffer his Crucifixion as shown in their faces. His own face shows shock at the view of the cross. The nails are driven in again with focus on the first strike of the hammer. Jesus is bloody, nude, and open to the direct derision of bystanders.

He asks God to forgive them. A storm begins. As depicted, however, it is not a storm of divine judgment. Rather, to judge by the lack of reaction from the soldiers and crowd, the storm only happens for Jesus and to Jesus. It is the internal struggle of Jesus to find God. After the cry of godforsakenness, silence ensues. Jesus can no longer hear the crowds. He only hears Satan, now disguised as a guardian angel, a prepubescent girl, blond and speaking with an educated English accent. Our savior is American and by implication so is his God. The angel proceeds to tempt Jesus away from his task.

The extended temptation vision lasts for 36 minutes. Its duration and location lead us to believe that here, finally, will come the mythic and theological resolutions the film has demanded. We are disappointed in this, however.

Without doubt the sequence almost pornographically prioritizes the final temptation as one of sex. As the angel says, there is only one Woman, with many faces; the "Savior *comes* from embrace to embrace." And so, when Magdalene and her child die, it is natural that Jesus resorts to Mary and eventually her sister Martha to fulfill his sexuality.

The resolution, however, becomes less clear as the vision proceeds, especially by the appearance of Saul/Paul as the creator of Christianity. His characterization is that of a southern American evangelist preaching the resurrected Christ on the street corner by personal testimony to his vision of and conversion by Jesus. Here, *The Last Temptation of Christ* makes clear that the evangelical faith, attributed to Paul, is not the way forward for the American Christ.

The way forward seems to require two decisions. First, Jesus must resolve the problem of the flesh, Woman, sexuality, and desire for a settled existence by breaking it off, denying it any spiritual power. Second he must get back on the cross and complete the suffering that God demands. The difficulty of the movie is that it has so inverted the story of Jesus by substituting traditional images of the presence of God for the presence of Satan that a final climactic inversion will not work. To put it simply, does Jesus decide for God by going back to the cross, or is this the end game of a very crafty Satan? Even more confusing, are both God and Satan portrayed by the film as projections of Jesus' tortured psyche? Because the film has not developed a reliable camera perspective, we do not know how to understand the final act of Jesus. While Scorsese may well have intended that the film end conclusively with Jesus' decision to die and bring salvation, the film itself is flawed in accomplishing that goal.

HOLLYWOOD'S MAKING OF THE AMERICAN CHRIST

More than any other previous Hollywood production, *The Last Temptation of Christ* galvanized opposition even before its production.[1] Paramount, the original sponsor of the project, pulled out under pressure. Universal picked up the film and pushed for a quick completion under mounting opposition from Evangelicals and Catholics. Criticism focused on the explicit sexuality between Jesus and Magdalene. *The Last Temptation of Christ* made headlines and got a cover story in *Time* (August 15, 1988). The reaction illustrates what we can now see as a historical split in Hollywood's audience. *The Last Temptation of Christ*, like *Jesus Christ Superstar* before it, presumed the existence of a portion of the American audience who sought their Jesus outside the confines of church tradition. Unlike *Jesus Christ Superstar*, however, *The Last Temptation of Christ* no longer was able to bounce its interpretation off a well-established Protestant mainstream tradition. Instead, it used Hollywood's own tradition as the basis for its effect.

In this, *The Last Temptation of Christ* is the most academic and well-researched Jesus film in terms of its reading and awareness of prior Hollywood tradition. It is very aware of how Jesus has been treated by the great epic films of DeMille, Ray, and Stevens. It also appreciates the television production of Zeffirelli. It follows up on impulses and icons created by *Jesus Christ Superstar*. The references are so numerous that on each new viewing new shots or allusions emerge. *The Last Temptation of Christ* is the first Hollywood production of the American Christ that swims almost exclusively in the world of Hollywood mythic tradition.

From the opening titles (in a technique begun by *King of Kings* [1927]), the viewer is directed to the emphases of the movie. As we have seen, however, the traditional theological issue of the dual substance of Christ is quickly eroded. The dual substance becomes truncated from a complex mythic duality of flesh and spirit to the American and physically loaded terms of male and female. That line of thought results in an overt rejection of comfortable American suburbia, for this Christ does not lead toward family and fatherhood.

The movie is an exploration of a male psyche. In the film's terminology the World of God is the object of the quest of the Christ. The quest is an intrapsychic, visionary one. The film seldom allows us to see conclusively that the supernatural has reality outside of the tortured imaginings of Jesus. This interior turn in the Cinematic Savior may have been presaged by his treatment in *Jesus Christ Superstar*, but there it remains less interior in the sense of psychological terrors and more in the realm of existential decision. Jesus in *Jesus Christ Superstar* remains a man of complete faith even in the face of absolute temptation to deny God, who clearly still exists.

In *The Last Temptation of Christ*, nothing exists except Christ and his experience. Cinematically, this is accomplished by an early identification of the camera perspective as the same as Jesus' own retelling of his story. If there is clear indication of resurrection in *The Last Temptation of Christ* then it must lie in Christ's narration of the film. Therefore, the land-scape, the mise-en-scene of the film, mirrors his own internal state. By its use of soundtrack, and the casting of the crowds, the film makes this Christ alien to us. Palestine is a burned-out shell, a desert, populated by Africans and Mediterraneans. They are accompanied by a world music with Latin American and African accents. The scene, surreal throughout, serves as a mythic backdrop to the story of Jesus and his disciplines. All of them are American with a tendency toward Brooklyn/East Coast accents. The opponents, supernatural or human, are always stereotyped as English. Jesus' psyche is that of a classic agonistic American hero. The Christ sees himself as isolated on the dramatic stage of his mythic soul. The daring development here is in locating this American hero not on the epic stage of an Americanized reading of world history, but inside himself. In this sense, the film in its totality constructs late twentieth-century America as the tortured Christ. His delusions are ours. His choices become those presented at a great turning point in American culture.

This unsettling vision of ourselves, totally against our own images of our secure place as God's chosen on earth, makes the film most shocking at a deep mythological level. Its lack of a conclusive resolution to the theological problems posed exposes the viewer to the darkest possibilities. The transcendent mission that we have been following is itself in signifi-cant doubt. We are a delusional people who no longer have the capacity to formulate coherent theology, let alone a national mission statement.

To say that this was Scorsese's intent goes beyond what we can glean of direct historical evidence surrounding the film and its creators. A direct historical interpretation must surely go no further than that suggested by Stern, Jefford, and DeBona.[2] They argue from the evidence of Scorsese's previous films that the movie intentionally plays against the tide of post-Vietnam Reagan America and the now well-recognized conservative recovery of the American self-image as the moral as well as political and military master of the world stage. Scorsese, in this view, read the times and constructed the film to employ the Hollywood tradition against its own conservative tendencies.

No American director can compare to Scorsese in intimate knowledge of film technique, and especially history. *The Last Temptation of Christ* shows his signature style and construction throughout. He constructs the film with perpetual homage to past Jesus films. His awareness of genre conven-tions and his ability to invert their intentions, to use them as the standard expectations of the audience, marks this film as the first Jesus film that constructs its iconography almost relentlessly out of reference to the Holly-wood tradition, unencumbered by broader controls of traditional Christian images. *The Last Temptation of Christ* yields to the best of avant-garde film impulses while remaining solidly within the Hollywood mainstream.

One of Scorsese's most notable inversions is the God shot. Only the opening scene and the scene of the circle in the desert contain direct overhead shots. As I noted above, they are sufficiently ambiguous that the perspective invoked by the camera is uncertain. While a heavenly–earthly axis is established, the perspective could be that of God or Jesus. Other than the overhead shot there is no clear presence of God in the circle scene, while it is clear that both Jesus and Satan are present. This leaves only the opening scene as possibly referring to God—not much to hang the film's theological hopes on. Notably few shots in the remainder of the film connect earth with heaven, which would reinforce the invocation of the divine. This lack of a clear axis deprives the viewer of a traditional convention around which the mythology of the film can be resolved into a coherent theology.

So when we are introduced, again from on high, to the circle of the Last Supper, we have a vague sense of unease. Here Scorsese's sacramental awareness becomes most explicit as Peter experiences the wine actually becoming blood. The supernatural and the mundane coincide effortlessly. The normal world is alive with power, and it appears directly in the sacramental elements. But, in the context of the entire film, the sacramental cannot even in this scene be clearly assigned to the power of God. So when Jesus arrives at Golgatha and experiences the death of forsakenness, the surreal quality of the staged event becomes clear. The cinematography, masterfully employed, allows for a close, visceral experience of the suffering of Jesus. But the suffering, visceral though it maybe, is difficult to connect with Jesus' voluntary self-sacrifice for our sins, the prophecy of Isaiah, seen only by Jesus notwithstanding.

The camera techniques, the choice to play always and everywhere against genre, the very pastiche nature of the film, which swirls and never resolves, leaves us wondering if the experiment is there merely for its own sake. Everything that *Jesus of Nazareth* did to establish seamless continuity in the life of Jesus, *The Last Temptation of Christ* undoes. This Jesus truly is a construct that represents postmodern, post-Christian America. The film offers no pathway for the ascent of the American soul, nor does it allow for the American projection of itself into the story of Jesus in order to construct itself as the mythic Christ who will save or is saving the world. Ultimately, *The Last Temptation of Christ* denies both strands of the Cinematic Savior tradition. America must confront its own confusion, its own psychosis in the person of its Christ.

Therefore, unlike every other Cinematic Savior, the Christ of *The Last Temptation of Christ* cannot be theologized, cannot be made to validate a view of God and God's relationship to the human. He is not the triumphant gnostic American Christ within each human liberated to return to his true home in the heavens. Nor is he an anti-gnostic American Savior who takes on true humanity for a time in order to save the world and chart a path to true perfection. Perhaps in this *The Last Temptation of Christ* was limited by a surviving and nagging orthodoxy that could not associate itself directly, as required by the Cinematic Savior tradition, with the national aspirations of America. Instead *The Last Temptation of Christ* sought to address from an American perspective the ancient and highly traditional dichotomy between the eternal and the historical. By reducing its images to the body (female) and the spirit (male) set in the midst of American film conventions, *The Last Temptation of Christ* could find no satisfying mythic resolution and therefore left us with the problem. In the process, God and theology disappear.

The need for a Cinematic Savior expressive of the American Christ will be addressed one more time. In it, the cinematography will relentlessly interpret Isaiah once again. A coherent vision and theology will emerge. Mel Gibson's *The Passion of the Christ* draws its iconic power and mythmaking force from the tradition of the Cinematic Savior, especially *The Last Temptation of Christ*. But it also invokes another tradition, one that transcends a number of film genres that I will now examine for their contribution from outside the Jesus tradition. For only by turning to the genre films that have succeeded in capturing and reflecting back America's vision of itself can we address a question drawn from the Hollywood tradition of the Cinematic Savior, a question that encapsulates America's desire to see itself as an action savior: How does Jesus get a gun?

7

———◆✦◆———

HOW JESUS GOT A GUN

WHY DOES JESUS NEED A GUN?

Had the Jesus of previous Hollywood versions been faithfully and fundamentally based on scriptural and other traditional religious sources and little else, we would not have become used to so much embroidery, editing, and variation in the evolution of representations of Jesus, and the Christ figure would not so easily or so manifestly have become a stand-in for America's own idealized version of itself. Hollywood's making of the Cinematic Savior includes, however, not only the incorporation of previous "authentic" versions of the Jesus story, but also obvious influences from other film genres and stories.

Tracing the course of this development, we have seen how the character of Jesus has increasingly become a truly human protagonist with real self-doubts. The reality of his self-doubt is expressed most recently either existentially—is there a knowable God out there?—or psychologically—who are these voices in my head? These human elements stand in the Hollywood tradition of the Cinematic Savior alongside images of the divine nature of the Christ. In order to understand fully the nature of the Cinematic Savior as the American hero who emerges in Gibson's *The Passion of the Christ*, however, we will need to cast a slightly wider net at other film traditions that might not at first glance strike us as the repository of images of Jesus. My brief detour from Jesus films here is prompted by the singular effect of *The Passion of the Christ* on the viewer.

How is it that after unrelenting focus on the brutal scourging, suffering, and Crucifixion, which is to say the utter defeat of Jesus physically, the viewer emerges from the theatre with a sense of militant triumph? This clear, visceral response to the last scene of the film stands in sharp contrast to the theme of the Messiah suffering for our sins established in the first frame by quotation of Isaiah 53. The myth and style of Hollywood films, especially as found in epics, Westerns, and science fiction provide the palette of icons upon which *The Passion of the Christ* depends for its final effective reversal. The contemporary audience has been prepared by the conventions of Hollywood to see Jesus as an American action hero because Hollywood had early on already hybridized the Christ myth within genre films of heroic American action in order to bring forth a peculiarly American brand of hero. Not surprisingly, then, the American Christ emerges from *The Passion of the Christ* to lead the world in a way previously unseen in the history of the Cinematic Savior.

A full treatment of the history of the American hero in Hollywood film would require another full-length book. Here, however, it suffices to describe a certain type of American hero who represents America as we prefer to see ourselves on the world stage. The ideal for heroic America is a man of peace who prefers the security of home, family, friends, and community. He only abandons this life when forced to by an overwhelming evil outside of his control. Only then, and frequently only after nearly being killed most sadistically, does he use violence to right wrongs, avenge the weak, and restore the world to its proper peaceful order.

Recognizable here is the Christ who suffers for our sins, dies, and is resurrected to the heavens. According to Christian biblical tradition he will return at the end of time to battle evil and judge the wicked and the good. In Hollywood film this last element is no longer a final end-of-time visitation by the returning Christ, but now becomes a mundane and violent vengeance that restores the current order to justice. The end-of-time visitation of Christ can be played out again and again by thoroughly human American heroes.

In this hero's story violent revenge for past wrongs can be taken somewhat reluctantly. Violence is seen as justified by the extreme circumstances. And the circumstances according to the well-established Hollywood formula frequently involve sex, sadism, and melodrama. The American audience sees itself participating in necessary violence, sometimes even extremely graphic violence, as long as the cause is sufficient and the violence of the revenge fits the crime. Even occasionally sadistic excesses on the part of the hero may be understandable to the American audience, especially if he takes no real pleasure in them. The American action hero allows the audience a catharsis of its own violent desire for revenge within the safe haven of the filmic world. By showing the hero engaged in protecting the weak (women, children, and particularly dogs), the catharsis of revenge moves to a higher key of justice.

The Hollywood Jesus movies avoid showing Jesus as righteous judge. Only in *Jesus Christ Superstar* and *The Last Temptation of Christ* does he break a sweat when he cleanses the temple, and even there the scenes are brief. God's own judgment at the Crucifixion occurs only in the form of storm and earthquake in two films: *King of Kings* (1927) and *The Passion of the Christ*. Indeed, within the biblical tradition itself the full depiction of Christ as judge and warrior occurs only in Revelation (The Apocalypse of John). In Revelation dramatic resolution of mythic images occurs in the final battle of good versus evil. Those battle scenes are driven by heavenly armies, ultimately led by Christ on the one side and Satan on the other. Christ's icon is that of the warlike Lamb of God, an inversion of image that contradicts both the terms of warrior and of lamb. Satan, true to form, occurs as a massive dragon. Judgment and justice in Revelation are reserved to the Christ at the end of time. They are denied to any human agency or institution.

As the quintessential American mythmaker through two world wars and numerous other armed conflicts, Hollywood becomes the creative agent as America examines its own use of violence and how that relates to the peaceful claims of its own Christ. Deft creative sidesteps take the Jesus story into other genres, demythologizing the final apocalyptic judgment of biblical tradition and displacing its sadism into the personal life of the American hero. He bears the duties of not only sufferer, but also final judge. Ultimately, the American hero as Christ bearer will become a Christ figure himself, and as such may be justifiably driven to pick up a gun. When, then, we come to the most sadistic of the Jesus films, *The Passion of the Christ*, it evokes not only the Jesus film tradition but deftly references the style and content of numerous heroic action films in Hollywood history.

In plotting out the trajectory that Hollywood has traced in preparing its viewers for the transformation of sacrificial lamb into the warrior Lamb of God, I have chosen representatives of three genres as a means of illustration: epics, Westerns, and science-fiction. I am confident that the examples could be multiplied.

TWO 1950S EPICS AS CHRIST BEARERS

Before its cinemascope, Technicolor release in 1959, *Ben-Hur* had already established itself as a crowd pleaser both in twentieth-century theatre and in silent film. Let it be said at the outset that *Ben-Hur* is in no way a Christ figure film: Its hero is not depicted as a Christ, but rather as a Jew who ultimately must be saved to a life of peace at the Crucifixion of Jesus. Judah Ben-Hur (Charlton Heston) embodies a satisfying American hero who can do violence in pursuit of revenge and justice and then abandon that life to become a peaceful Christian householder.

The movie presents Judah Ben-Hur as the new American. His story is integrated with the story of the Christ. The overture shows us Michelangelo's *Creation of Adam*. The first scene depicts the birth of Christ. The second scene introduces Ben-Hur. Although Judah is ostensibly a Jew, only clothing and a brief bow to Jewish customs mark him as Jewish. He is the quintessential homeowner in the American suburbs. All he lacks is Christ. This movie is the story of how he gains Christ.

Judah is a man of peace torn from his serene home life and sold into slavery by his friend, a Roman named Masala. The quest of Judah, through slavery and shipwreck, is for vengeance. When he has satisfied that vengeance in the famous chariot race, Judah goes home. It is important that Judah does not have to kill his enemy, Masala, directly. Instead the movie implies that the divine hand judges Masala for his villainy and treachery when Masala is fatally injured in the chariot race. In his final scene with Masala, Judah forgivingly states, "I see no enemy." The hero has his justice. The enemy is eliminated, no blood falls on our hero, and he forgives.

That Christ is behind Judah's salvation in the arena becomes clear in the second climax of the movie. Judah finds his sister and mother in a leper colony and witnesses the Via Dolorosa and Crucifixion, during which it becomes clear that Judah is converted. The Crucifixion becomes a model for later Crucifixions in Jesus movies, notably in *King of Kings* (1961) and *The Greatest Story Ever Told*. Most importantly, any identification of the storm or earthquake as the judgment of God is muted in favor of the healing rain that literally washes away the marks of leprosy from Judah's mother and sister. Jesus takes the world of our sins unto himself and through his blood purifies the very earth. The character who dramatically and effectively receives this salvation for all of us is Judah, who now returns to a life of Christian peace to live happily ever after with Esther.

Ben-Hur illustrates the pattern of epic American Hero. As embodied by him, America, who loves only a peaceful home, is unjustly oppressed, enslaved, and nearly dies (shipwreck) only to be resurrected through water with a strong motivation for vengeance. By struggle and heroic action, America seeks revenge. The art of the film is in the direction by William Wyler. He presents huge spectacle, with satisfying catharsis, while at the same time making sure America is saved by Jesus from enacting its own vengeance. His cinematography, style, and pace influence contemporary epics. Watch *Ben-Hur* and then watch *Lord of the Rings* to see the close relationship in style. We have in *Ben-Hur* the story of an American action hero who, after he has fulfilled his quest, converts once again to peace. He, like the America he represents, is allowed the pursuit of righteous vengeance and its satisfaction before conversion to the Christ of peace. Jesus hasn't yet gotten a gun, but Jesus saves the American who stands up for himself and his family.

Directed by Stanley Kubrick and starring Kirk Douglas, *Spartacus* is among the last and maybe the greatest of the ancient epic spectaculars. It far surpasses more recent attempts such as *Gladiator* and *Troy* at reclaiming the genre. *Spartacus* postulates its hero as an obvious forerunner to Christ and as the precursor and model for a righteous America, whose Christ will lead the Union armies to free the black slaves of the South. The opening voice-over narration of the film reminds the viewer that Christianity, not the hordes of barbarians, will overthrow Rome. Rome here is a stand-in for the slave culture of the American South. It also has connections to the American fight for freedom from England. Kubrick has used the standard Hollywood conventions: Aristocratic Romans (Charles Laughton, Lawrence Olivier, Peter Ustinov) speak aristocratic English, while Spartacus (Kirk Douglas) is thoroughly American.

The slave rebellion in *Spartacus* is a full-blown class action against injustice. The film highlights the personal saga of the hero while at the same time showing by intercuts, crowd scenes, and small vignettes the huge community of slaves, who are nevertheless individualized for the viewer. For example, after the final battle scene we are allowed to recognize among the dead family groups, children, and old people who have been highlighted earlier in the film.

Spartacus himself is depicted as the natural human being: Although uneducated, he is thirsty for knowledge; although born a slave, his morals surpass those of his owners. Spartacus is galvanized into action against oppression by the heroic death of a black slave who refuses to slay him in the arena for the pleasure of Roman aristocrats and who turns instead on the aristocrats themselves. The fact that he is the only black among a group of slave gladiators of white and European origin ensures that the American audience need not overcome any racial prejudices in order to identify with the slave population. It is remarkable that while a black man initiates the heroic rebellion, the remainder of the film is virtually devoid of a black presence. The black slave killed by Crassus (Olivier) is hung upside down as a warning to the others not to attempt a similar rebellion. So *Spartacus* invokes the holy American war against slavery while transferring the experience of enslavement from African Americans to the European immigrant experience.

As the film unfolds, Spartacus accumulates a large share of Hollywood epic hero traditions. For example, the film evokes strong parallels to DeMille's *The Ten Commandments*. The slave community is shown as a veritable mirror of U.S. immigration in the early decades of the twentieth century. Look closely to see typical movie types of Irish, Eastern European, and Italian faces. Like Moses and the children of Israel, they seek to flee by way of the sea.

The evocation of Moses—cinematically a charismatic man of action, war, and nation building—gives way to Spartacus, the heroic Christ. As he is crucified, Spartacus is visited by Verinia (Jean Simmons), his wife, with their newborn son. "He is free," she says of the son as she embraces Spartacus' feet. This final scene reverses the tragedy planned by Crassus. Spartacus after death on the cross was to have been burned and his ashes scattered in secret to ensure that his memory would disappear. Instead, he attains apotheosis and immortality by fathering a freeborn heir who will know and carry on the story. The filmic language fosters an iconography unmistakably parallel to Jesus and in some ways more complete. Hung in the air on an axis connecting the earth and the heavens, Spartacus becomes the focus of mythic resolutions between slavery and freedom, death and fertility. His resolutions are specific American additions to the Christ myth. The holy family escapes slavery. Spartacus, unlike Jesus, dies having known the pleasure of home, hearth, children, and a good woman. As did Judah Ben-Hur, he has a family, including a beautiful child. The American Christ takes up arms when forced, by overwhelming evil and overwhelming odds, to defend his liberty and the liberty of the weak, to fight for truth and justice and freedom. The Cinematic Savior, who is America, saves us all and is infinitely capable of Resurrection as needed.

It is difficult to underestimate the influence of *Spartacus* on the Cinematic Savior. If movies had marketed action figures in 1960, then we would have a Spartacus figure in our pantheon. In Spartacus, the American Christ receives action hero status. He can do so because he is not Jesus, but yet he bears the mythological images of the Christ. *Braveheart* will retell virtually the same story, winning four Academy Awards including best picture and best director. Mel Gibson, who starred in and directed *Braveheart,* will go on to apply the same cinematic and mythmaking techniques to Jesus in *The Passion of the Christ.*

Hollywood's making of the American Christ allows for recombinations of traditions in filmmaking to satisfy the need to see America as the vindicated suffering hero, the hero who suffers for his family so that all might live in peace with theirs.

THE WESTERN

The genre into which America has most consistently projected itself and from which America has much of its heroic self-image is the Western. At its apex in the 1950s and 60s, the Western constructed the perfect fictional analogue to American culture. In the Western we find the patterning of the American hero. Not surprisingly, he comes to take on superhuman qualities. Like Spartacus, he becomes a demythologized Christ who is remythified as the super-personality of America. This development is best illustrated by three films beginning with *Shane* (1953) and its remakes as *High Plains Drifter* (1973) and *Pale Rider* (1985).

In *Shane*, directed by George Stevens, the gunfighter with a bloody past puts down his gun to live peacefully with a churchgoing farm family in a Wyoming valley. Unfortunately, the farmers are at war with cattlemen, whom they have displaced from the land. In the process of the movie, Shane (Alan Ladd) befriends the Starrets: Joe, Marion, and Joey, almost seduces (or is seduced by) Marion, and becomes the heroic friend of Joey, their son. He is forced by Jack Wilson (Jack Palance), the hired gun of the cattlemen, to strap on his own gun in order to save the farmers and ensure justice on the American frontier. The film ends with Shane, wounded, riding off into the mountains while the young child cries after him in the street.

As hero, Shane embodies the American ideal. He is a reluctant hero who takes up the gun only when justice for the weak, or in this case, those unskilled at gunplay, is at stake. He suffers beatings and humiliation, almost beyond human endurance. In this depiction of suffering, the casting of Ladd, with his slight frame and choirboy good looks, emphasizes even further the brutality and ugliness of raw primitive male violence. Only in the final gunfight does he triumph. The film leaves open the possibility that he dies as a result of his wounds.

So much for the mundane development of the plot. Cinematically, however, this film remythologizes America (which had recently won a world war, and was currently fighting the Cold War) into a savior figure. Shane, his wounded arm hanging at his side, rides into the sunset, but more significantly up into the mountains, out of which we saw him ride in the opening scene. The descent from and ascent back into the mountains brackets the entire film. He has come from the wild and returns to the wild. He wears his fringed buckskin shirt in each scene. The fringe stands in for angels wings as well as evoking the primitive man. In his time as a farmer, he dresses in more conventional jeans and flannel shirt. His descent and ascent parallel Moses, who descends from Sinai with the

Law and ascends Sinai to die. But, more importantly, Shane's descent and ascent act as a visual parallel to the descent and ascent of the Christ, who comes from the heavens to bring justice to the earth and ascends again to the right hand of the Father. The trajectory of Shane mirrors the historical incarnation of Jesus as the Prince of Peace, and in his final scene Shane also embodies the functions of the Christ, the Lamb of God who ensures justice at the end of time. Here, though, the last battle is simply the final battle of the film.

This is not to say that Shane is intended as a Christ in every respect (although we should bear in mind that Stevens, who directed *Shane*, would direct *The Greatest Story Ever Told* 12 years later). It is simply to say that the figure of Shane is an embodiment of heroic America who fulfills the roles of both messiah of peace and of righteous judgment during the movie. In *Shane*, the American Christ has a gun.

By the 1970s the image of the heroic gunfighter had been to a large extent reversed by the anti-hero of the "spaghetti" Westerns. Many of these were actually remakes of the samurai films of Akira Kurosawa but given a peculiar American twist with Clint Eastwood as star and such titles as *A Fistful of Dollars* and *A Few Dollars More*. The cigar smoking anti-hero in Eastwood's interpretation was a hired gun with a very seedy past who by and large spent the movie surviving, his mere survival a testimony to the futility of making sense out of a senselessly violent time.

In the first remake of *Shane*, however, Eastwood as director and star goes even beyond this anti-hero image, making *High Plains Drifter* into a direct reversal of almost every image in Shane. The Stranger rides up out of the heat (hell) onto the level of the town. At the end of the film he rides back down into the heat. He dresses in a long black coat. In the case of Shane, the buckskins with their fringes substitute for the wings of an archangel. The Stranger presents a similar substitution, his long black coat a substitution for the wings of an avenging angel sent back from death to exact punishment on those who betrayed and killed Sheriff Duncan. *The Matrix* uses the long black coat similarly to suggest both the superhero's cape and angelic wings.

The Stranger rapes Callie, the town tease, who it turns out played a pivotal role in the death of Duncan. Even though the scene suggests that she wanted to be raped and actually enjoyed it, the rape functions as an act of judgment against her. The Stranger systematically kills those sent against him. He avoids death itself, because as we learn, he is already dead. The town itself is painted red and renamed from Largo to Hell as part of the judgment against them. Instead of a cute Joey, we get a dwarf, the butt of every town joke, who becomes mayor if only for a day. By these consistent reversals, the exposure of every sin of the "godfearin" towns-people forces a reconsideration of the America conventionally projected by previous Westerns.

And yet, the classic American narrative underlies the film and emerges to guarantee America's view of its true self. The revelation may come a bit late, but as the flashback and dream sequences make clear the Stranger is the avenging angel of Sheriff Duncan. The Stranger confirms this in the final frames of the film when he points out to the dwarf that the dead in unmarked graves never rest.

In the story of Duncan the standard elements of the Cinematic Savior show up. He was brutally and sadistically beaten to death with a bullwhip while the town looked on and did nothing to help. The Stranger even bears the stigmata of the whip on his neck. His death then must be quite graphi-cally and precisely avenged. The townspeople must re-experience their own sins in their own constructed hell. Like that of Dante's *Inferno*, the retribution is sadistic, at times funny, and intended to redress the imbalance to the divine and human order created by human cowardice and sin.

In the style of Hollywood, while the hero has become supernatural, the vengeance he exacts remains realistic and individualized. We have a remythologizing of the hero, now supernatural and returned from the place where unjustly murdered heroes go. We have also, however, the realization of judgment not in final, supernatural terms, but in the mun-dane world of realistic film.

The transference of Christ symbols to the hero with a gun emerges clearly with its implications for America and its self-consciousness. We remain downtrodden, bloodied, even, as expressed here, dead, but we always get up (or are resurrected) for the sake of our own vengeance. No action hero in American film remains dead. America is the downtrodden hero who cannot die.

The depiction of retributive justice, like all violence in film, became more primal and overtly sadistic by 1975. Sex, sadism, and melodrama came more fully forward, especially after the demise of the production code. The turn toward realistic film was actually an incorporation of style and film technique pioneered in gothic horror films, film noir, and particularly associated with porn. Realism becomes increasingly asso-ciated with gruesome, lurid special effects reducing both the physical and spiritual suffering to a single shot or series of shots.[1] In *High Plains Drifter* this type of realism is relentless from frame to frame, sequence to sequence, the spiritual and physical sadism combining powerfully and uncomfortably with their justification borrowed from the Jesus story. Jesus is back, he has a gun, and he is meting out justice.

This same realism drives *The Passion of the Christ*. The film technique that is heir to the same traditions as *High Plains Drifter* ensures a set of associations for the viewer. We know that Jesus, as action hero, will get up from the brutal scourging and sooner or later come back to mete out justice with a "gun." As America, he is crucified by our enemies and will come back to destroy them.

The final remake of *Shane*, *Pale Rider*, returns to the mythical pattern of *Shane* itself and retains the supernaturalism of *High Plains Drifter*. This time the Preacher (Clint Eastwood) comes out of the mountains to avenge the death of a young girl's dog.

The supernatural and apocalyptic nature of the film is almost too heavy-handed. The farm families of *Shane* have now become prospectors, run out and murdered by a proto-corporate, environmentally unfriendly mining operation. The eight-year-old Joey has now become a fourteen-year-old girl, Morgan, who falls in love with the Preacher. His arrival out of the mountains is in direct response to prayer. She identifies him at the dinner table by reading Rev 6:7–8. He is the Pale Rider whose name is Death. He has six bullet holes in his back. Like the Stranger in *High Plains Drifter* he is a resurrected human with stigmata, sent back from the grave to protect the weak and exact precise retribution for his own murder. Unlike the Stranger, his descent from the mountains and ascent back connects him with the same cycle of mythic associations begun by Shane. Here we have the apocalyptic reappearance of the Christ at the final hour, neatly sidestepped by refashioning him into an American hero. Without doubt the Preacher is sent by God. The supernatural has returned full force to American cinema by 1985. And Jesus still has a gun.

The return of the Christ predicted by Revelation now has been grafted onto the American Western with its heroic tradition. This allows for a full exploration of the Christ myth—life, death, Resurrection, and return for judgment—without the theological problems attendant upon a direct representation of Jesus. The American Christ can carry the aspirations of America as idealized America without being weighed down with the charges of blasphemy or sacrilege. The American hero, now supernaturalized, can bear the actual stigmata of his unjust death and burial in an unmarked grave. The transference of important elements of the Jesus story cannot be missed. The creation of the American heroic Christ, who not only suffers and dies at the hands of the evil enemies of true America but also returns to deliver us from evil and to judge those evil men who have done us wrong, captures the desire of America to see itself as victim and victor on the national and world stage.

THE SHIFT TO SCIENCE FICTION FANTASY

While the Western began to fade as the primary genre for American self-actualization, Science Fiction Fantasy replaced it. Eastwood filmed the eulogy of the Western in *Unforgiven* (1992). The sci-fi genre gathered a variety of stylistic elements together in its own development. Not surprisingly, it often reprises the Christ myth and Jesus story.

Stylistically, the high modern, absolutely clean Protestant style of Stanley Kubrick's *2001: A Space Odyssey* expresses an internal spiritual impulse that is picked up by *Star Wars* (1976). And *Blade Runner* sets the standard for dystopian depiction of the degraded modern mise-en-scene. While both contain enough biblical allusions to warrant their own studies as religious masterpieces, neither has a clear allusion to Jesus or the Christ.

In the heyday of UFO spottings sci-fi produced an almost allegorical Jesus film with *The Day the Earth Stood Still* (1951). An alien, Klaatu, from another planet, who goes under the assumed name of Carpenter, comes to Washington, DC, as a prince of peace to warn U.S. officials that their arms race will lead to their own destruction. For his trouble he is imprisoned, killed, and resuscitated by Gort, his faithful robot guardian. Before he ascends back into the heavens via flying saucer, he warns the earthlings that if they do not change their ways, his civilization will return to destroy them. The entire Christ myth, including the promise of return for final judgment, is transferred in *The Day the Earth Stood Still* to the supposedly nonmythological realm of real science. While the Christ himself never gets a gun, it is clear that Gort or those like him will fulfill the roles traditionally reserved for the archangels in the final battle as described in Revelation.

The Matrix (1999) concludes the cycle of films in which Jesus gets a gun. It combines numerous styles derived from Westerns, film noir, epic, and of course the now well-established sci-fi genre. That Neo, aka John Anderson (Keanu Reeves), is a Jesus figure, a Christ, is writ so large throughout the movie that, again, it almost becomes blatantly allegorical. He is "The One," a direct quotation from *The Greatest Story Ever Told*. Neo is an anagram for one. He is resurrected by Trinity, a stand-in for God, now interpreted as a woman. Neo: "I thought you were a guy. . . ." Trinity: "Most guys do."

He dies with the stigmata of bullet holes apparent out of his back as Smith shoots him in the matrix. The visual links him to the Preacher in *Pale Rider*. The coloration and angle of key shots evoke comparison with Zeffirelli's *Jesus of Nazareth*. See particularly the dramatic kiss of Trinity to bring Neo back to life in comparison with the shot of Mary the Mother as she cradles Jesus at the foot of the cross in *Jesus of Nazareth*.

With his enhanced martial arts powers inside the matrix, Neo is the ultimate Christ become the ultimate action hero. Only in a final act of postresurrection self-realization does he overcome the gun and stop the bullets in mid-air. Even here the pose, palm outstretched, reminds the viewer of Superman. Of course we have seen him perform some of the most elegant on-screen mayhem with a gun prior to this scene of enlightenment, so the movie suggests that through life comes salvation from life and through violence salvation from violence. The violence itself is further removed from normal reality by the film conceit that the enemy is really an evil-machine empire that has generated a virtual world.

Finally, Neo even saves Agent Smith, a program in the matrix, by union with him. This last we will discover fully only in the two subsequent movies. While *The Matrix* may fold in Eastern religious traditions, especially Taoism, Buddhism, and Hinduism, it remains dominated by the Hollywood tradition of the Cinematic Savior. In the *Matrix* trilogy the American Christ and his cohort endure sadism, and in the hero's case, a final crucifixion, while never ending the cycle of violence and sadism or betrayal. In its underlying myth, then, the *Matrix* trilogy shows us repeatedly the American Christ with a gun, the ultimate action hero. Neo suffers, dies, and is resurrected to fight the evil empire of the machines for the sake of the preservation of Zion (a symbol of true America) buried deep within the earth. Zion is a primal Christian society where the effervescence of the spirit of freedom fills the traditional charismatic Christian role of possession by the Holy Spirit. See here the "Rave" scene in *Matrix Reloaded*.

By projecting the Christ into a dystopian postapocalyptic future where humans are enslaved as the personal batteries of machines, the film allows for the safe examination of the American present. In that present, the Cinematic Savior has found a gun, and the audience expects him to use it. It may be that at this point in Hollywood history sci-fi provides the most trouble-free catharsis for America. It provides a safe and creative world of reference unencumbered by claims for authenticity. Sci-fi only requires that a movie set up clear rules and remain true to them.

After all, if you make historical epics, especially of Jesus, you always will have to contend with scholars and religious types who will dispute or carp about authenticity. In sci-fi we now have a speculative future world where we can recombine our traditional mythic elements and make up our own rules for their balancing. Does Christ need a woman? You can give him one as a romantic, even sexual, interest. Does he need a gun to fulfill the American desire for rough justice and revenge? OK. As long as his myth remains, however subdued or hidden, it draws on the deep cultural currents of America. He can both be Savior of the internal man and Savior from external enemies foreign or domestic. His content is always America. And because his myth is so well structured and repeated across several Hollywood genres, the least suggestion of the Cinematic Savior, the American Christ, requires his conclusive victory, which victory, more often than not, also requires a gun.

THE AMERICAN CHRIST AND *THE PASSION OF THE CHRIST*

Elements of the life and theology of Christ reverberate through the career of Mel Gibson. Even his early Australian film career samples the hero myth as *Gallipoli* and the three *Mad Max* movies make clear. This tradition is further developed in the police action hero of the four *Lethal Weapon* films. Gibson plays a Vietnam veteran, psychologically disturbed by his wife's murder, who endures and metes out sadistic violence. Ultimately his redemption is in the discovery of family and fatherhood.

In Gibson's directing career we have only to point out *Braveheart*. The tale of William Wallace parallels strongly the story of Spartacus, or of our prototypical heroic Christ with a gun. William Wallace, a peaceful Scottish farmer, is transformed by the unjust murder of his wife into a military genius, savage warrior, and leader of the Scottish revolution against the English. Ultimately he is captured by Edward Longshanks, King of England, tortured, and drawn and quartered with the cry of freedom on his dying lips.

The film's style reprises all the high notes of classic Hollywood epic, but especially, I think, Kubrick's direction of *Spartacus*. The final sequence, in which Wallace is wheeled in a cart with the cross-beam of his future "Crucifixion" bound to his shoulders, establishes Wallace as the Christ of Scotland.

While *Braveheart* is set in Scotland, its hero is thoroughly developed according to the conventions of the Cinematic Savior. The movie takes the realistic tendency in film to new levels in its depiction of battle and especially the evidently sexual pleasure taken in sadistic torture. Wallace, however, remains above pleasure in another world of righteous revenge and justice. He embodies the American ideal of righteous vengeance: necessary, savage, and dispassionate. With this movie, Gibson as director perfects his own formula of sex, sadism, and melodrama. His attention to verisimilitude provides the lay audience with an authentic look, despite the fact that scholars of Scottish history would take strong exception to many of the elements the film provides interpretatively.

The Patriot utilizes the same formula and style; this time the main character is driven to violence by the murder of his son. Similarly, Gibson provides verisimilitude in pursuit of authenticity, but was nevertheless accused by historians of playing fast and loose with the facts. Here the American hero occurs in all his glory fighting against the savage and sadistic British to avenge the unjust murder of his son.

What *Braveheart* and *The Patriot* lack, however, is an exploration of the darker world of sex, sadism, and revenge provided by the film noir or gangster film. This element, especially in its cinematic coloration or palette, shows up in another film in which Gibson starred, but did not direct, *Payback* (1999). As in *High Plains Drifter* the anti-hero is explored now in hyperrealistic fashion. The major style of the movie is a hyperreal gritty blue tone meant to evoke the grainy black and white of classic film noir. It is also used to good effect by Stephen Spielberg (and Stanley Kubrick) in *AI* to indicate a situation of hyperreality in which the audience is given to know that this level of reality is the truth that lies behind our normal mundane experience. Spielberg also uses it to excellent effect in *Minority Report*.

Payback is a study in sadism reaching a climax in the "hammer and toes" scene in which Porter (Gibson) is forced to reveal where he is holding the crime boss's son. By close-up reaction shots the scene alternates between Porter's pain and the sexual, orgasmic delight of his torturers. We have already been given the close tie between sadism, sex, and orgasm in the on-screen S and M relationship between Pearl (Lucy Liu) and Gregg (Val Resnick).

Despite the fact that Porter himself is a small-time hood and con-man, he reprises the major elements of the American hero, thereby almost becoming identifiable as a Christ. The echoes are so strong that the conclusion is inevitable at some level. Porter is shot by his wife and left for dead, while she runs off with his best friend Gregg. He doesn't die, however, and comes back not so much for revenge as for the $60,000 his partner has stolen from him. The film is the story of his repeated attempts to gain his fair cut from the mob, which of course would rather kill him than pay. By the end of the film he walks away with $130,000. In the process he exacts precise and necessary retribution. There is even a pseudo-resurrection scene near the end of the film shot as an escape from the trunk of a car.

What is fascinating about the film is that it never really shows you the actual act of torture; instead, it shows you reactions. The unseen is as sinister and evocative as the seen. The film noir crime thriller has been pushed by director Brian Helgeland to its ultimate inversion, and the anti-hero becomes the dark inversion of the American Christ. Porter appeals to us because once again we see, however inverted, the myth of America, unjustly tortured, self-sacrificing, and getting up from a terrible beating to gain justice along with vengeance. Porter is not a Christ, but he evokes enough of the American Christ myth to become appealing. The dark palette and the careful and repeated studies of sadism provide a catharsis for the audience. We appreciate the hero's dogged determination and resilience. The inversion works, because what can be better than finding the true American hero in the most unlikely of places? In this, of course, *Payback* follows a long line of crime films and great film criminals who become heroic figures, including *The Petrified Forest*, *Bonnie and Clyde*, and *Taxi Driver*.

HOLLYWOOD'S MAKING OF THE AMERICAN CHRIST

So how did Jesus get a gun? Jesus got a gun by a series of creative sidesteps within the process of Hollywood's perfecting the American hero. These sidesteps occurred naturally as Hollywood developed heroes to fit America. The fundamental structure of the Christ myth is broken apart and reassembled, but never directly attributed to the Jesus character. Hollywood has been happy to give us Jesus as the Christ who descends from the heavens, gathers disciples, teaches, works miracles, is betrayed, suffers unjustly at the hands of religious and political authorities, is crucified, dies, and is buried and resurrected to ascend to the heavens. It has not given us Jesus as the Warrior Lamb of God who returns to gather his elect and vanquish the evil forces that oppose him. The satisfaction of the final judgment instead has been provided by iconic heroes, never named Jesus, who are therefore free to explore at various points in their career the close connection assumed by America between justice and vengeance.

This complete, heroic American Christ can then reappear in a variety of genres. As he does so he accumulates to himself a variety of styles and significances that stay with the Hollywood audience. The heroic Christ will at some point get up from a terrible beating or even on-screen death to exact an acceptable vengeance on the evil perpetrators, his and (of course, for the fundamental process is one of identification) our enemies.

When, therefore, a new Jesus movie is released in this context of American cinematic tradition, the more we see him beaten, the more we see him suffer, the more we anticipate divine retribution to be exacted for those who cause him to suffer. The more realistic the film technique, the more we associate it with previous "realistic" genres and heroes, and the more sadism we can accept as part of the on-screen depiction.

Jesus depicted as the sadistically beaten action figure who survives to arrive at the cross may die for our sins, but he also dies to rise again and avenge our enemies, because Jesus is America. His enemies and ours are one and the same. The style, the camera perspective, the iconography are not exclusive to Jesus movies. They carry meaning established throughout the history of Hollywood film. Thus, when we see a blue palette it shows us the hyperreal, the reality behind mundane appearances. And when we see the realistic depiction of brutal torture, it references not only the scourgings of 30 c.e., but every unjust act of violence against an innocent America in cinema. The construction of the Cinematic Savior is now grounded in the broad electronic image tradition of Hollywood itself. This set of images defines the mythology and theology of America.

8

THE PASSION OF THE CHRIST: JESUS AS ACTION HERO

THE POST-9/11 SAVIOR

The film treatment of the Cinematic Savior, as we have seen in previous chapters, has been one of continual change, but also of the gradual accumulation of a set of visual symbols, common themes, and camera styles that form a tradition of their own. It is a tradition that we as viewers have naturalized and accepted as coming from a sacred space. We now arrive at the most recent on-screen incarnation of the Cinematic Savior. Although the critical analysis of a film becomes more and more difficult the closer its release date is to our own time and condition, let us try here to interpret Mel Gibson's *The Passion of the Christ* (2004) against the context established in previous chapters. For, given our review of the history of the Cinematic Savior, *The Passion of the Christ* truly references the Hollywood tradition as far back as DeMille. Gibson reaches all the way back to DeMille's silent film techniques and incorporates DeMille's emphasis on sadism and melodrama with elements from the whole of the Cinematic Savior tradition. Furthermore, Gibson is quite eclectic in borrowing from biblical and epic spectacular, Western, sci-fi, and crime genres in his cinematography, while adding to the Hollywood tradition with elements of pre-Vatican II Catholicism.

What is really in play here is America's sense of itself. And because the movie was released after 9/11, its new projection of the American Christ, now conceived of and shown as the ultimate action hero warrior, had powerful implications. If anything, this makes *The Passion of the Christ* a new icon for an America conceiving of itself as the Christ. The most striking departure from earlier versions lies, as its title suggests, in the fact that Gibson's established penchant for the extended treatment of sadistic violence may have prompted the narrowing of the film's scope to Jesus' final suffering and death. This precludes any coverage of his teaching or miracles. Even so, *The Passion of the Christ* can still draw on and continue a number of conventions already established for the Cinematic Savior, especially from the traditions of Zeffirelli and Scorsese.

THE CONTINUING SACRAMENTAL INTERPRETATION OF ISAIAH 53

Just as DeMille and Scorsese before him, Gibson opens with a title that directs the viewer as to how to view the movie:

He was wounded for our transgressions, crushed for our iniquities; by his wounds, we are healed (Isaiah 53).

As in *Jesus of Nazareth* and *The Last Temptation of Christ*, Isaiah 53 provides the final theology of the film. Since the film treats the story of Jesus' life only from Gethsemane to Resurrection, however, there are no other theological discussions of any significance in the film within its scope.

The film relentlessly demonstrates this fundamental point, which goes even further than Isaiah or for that matter any writing drawn from the New Testament: For every sin of the world, Jesus must be lashed, punched, kicked, brutalized, and humiliated. Just as importantly, the film asserts that this fact is good for the audience to watch. *The Passion of the Christ* weds theology and voyeurism into an overwhelmingly emotional audience experience. The film is so overwhelming in its examination of sadism that the audience may risk missing the pronounced, yet subtle, mythological and ideological alterations to the Jesus film tradition. The audience is so divided, perhaps even traumatized to a degree, by its responses that it may overlook the fundamental mythological message. Hence, many images lie latent. They return to us in later moments of contemplation and analysis. The film, however, draws on this scene in order to shape the audience's response to the last frame of the film, which depicts Jesus' movement out of the tomb after Resurrection.

The pivotal scene for the movie, approximately 12 minutes in length, is the scourging of Jesus. Only three of the four Gospels mention the scourging (Matt 27:26; Mark 15:15; John 19:1) and then only briefly. In each of the three Gospels Pilate is made directly responsible for the scourging. In each case no details are given and few words are used. Matthew and Mark: "having scourged Jesus" (two words in the Greek). John: "Then Pilate took Jesus and flogged him" (one word in the Greek). Matthew and Mark use the technical term for scourging, which was brutal punishment prescribed for capital offenders prior to crucifixion. John uses a less technical term. In John, the flogging of Jesus might be, as in the movie, an attempt to appease the high priests, and not regarded by Pilate as a precursor to crucifixion, but, while allowable, such an interpretation, is by no means clear from the text. In no case does the New Testament suggest that Pilate instructed the soldiers to soften the beating. Nor are the particulars of the scourging discussed. The Gospels themselves do not make the brutalization of Jesus a subject of theological or spiritual contemplation or enlightenment. In *The Passion of the Christ,* then, we see not an attempt at Gospel authenticity, but visual theological storytelling with a peculiar non-biblical emphasis dictated by directorial choice.

The scene brings together dramatically all of the major players in the death of Jesus for the film. The shock value of the scene lies not in the laceration or in the blood, but in the blood sport of the soldiers who in close-up portray the absolute and horrible delight of the true sadist. No subtitles provide us with the direct translation of the cruel and crude jokes made in street Latin about the victim. Sexual arousal on the part of the soldiers, however, is palpable. The viewer becomes uncomfortable at the least with this eroticization of violence done to Jesus. Even though American audiences have become used to Hollywood studies of sadism, they have never seen the motif so thoroughly applied to Jesus. In this way, Gibson fulfills DeMille's requirement of sex, sadism, and melodrama all in one scene. This scene not only establishes the literal, visual fulfillment of Isaiah 53, but also a scenario that demands a response according to the American heroic model.

Jesus remains silent, unbroken. At one critical juncture, apparently defeated and broken, he rises again in heroic defiance of their cruelty. This only rekindles the drive in the soldiers, who almost orgasm in their pleasure. Despite the explicitness of the violence and the delineation of the sadism of the soldiers, however, more than a human duel of wills has come to the fore here. No one except the Son of God, or a movie action hero, can survive the blood loss and the shock of this beating, which achieves a mythological, even metaphysical level.

Despite the visceral brutality the camera captures, the fundamental duel is a supernatural one. Satan circles the scene behind Caiaphas and then the soldiers, moving evil power from instigator to executioner.

We see Satan from Jesus' perspective. And we see Mary the Mother, also in close-up. The camera here and throughout the film unites her with her son in the duel between Jesus and Satan that began in the first scene of the film in the garden of Gethsemane. There Satan reminds Jesus that no one has ever been able to hold to the path that Jesus has chosen. Now, Jesus silently bears up under scourging; his real opponent is Satan.

The film structures the natural and supernatural world for the audience visually and morally. Hence, the soldier's sadism is intercut with Mary's suffering, compassion, and resolve. The audience, through Jesus' perspective, sees Satan carrying an ugly child, the Antichrist, as he moves about. Caiaphas, who originally was impelled to watch, becomes apparently sickened by what he has wrought and, one by one, he and his cronies turn away.

The scene ends with Abenader, who is Pilate's right arm, arriving to stop the beating. The soldiers have ignored Pilate's direct command and "killed" him. Unless you know, as we all know, that there is more, you would presume Jesus to be dead. As in action film, the apparently dead hero will be back. We are, after all, only a bit more than one hour into the film. The scourging establishes sets of dualities, a list of irresolvable opposites that will remain constant for the film. In keeping with action movie conventions, there are the good guys and the bad guys. The good guys are those sympathetic to the hero. The bad guys are those opposed. Clearly the good are Mary, Magdalene, and John the beloved disciple. The bad are equally obvious: Caiaphas and those with him who are aligned with Satan and the Antichrist child. These alignments will not change throughout the entire movie. They are two mythic poles. As myth the movie creates tension in two ways. How will future or present characters align themselves? How will the confrontation between the hero and the evil ones be resolved?

Because of the brutality of the scourging the audience aligns itself with Jesus, whether we regard him to be the Christ or not. Because of the mythic and iconic structure, which is informed both by previous Jesus movies and by American action hero movies, the audience must oppose his enemies. Because of the conventions of the action hero genre, the viewer anticipates justice and vengeance against the hero's enemies. No amount of disclaimer, exposition, or special pleading inside or outside the film can alter this structure unless, contrary to genre and therefore audience anticipation, Caiaphas and his henchmen convert, change, or repent of their wickedness. According to the formal conventions of the action movie genre, however, this would be unheard of. And so, unlike Caiaphas in *King of Kings* (1927), the bad guys in *The Passion of the Christ* do not repent. Nor, of course, can Satan. The appeals to genre established in the film control its theological possibilities. And in the final scenes of the movie, as in all action films, vengeance falls on them.

Left as ambiguous in their allegiances are the Romans. Somehow the film shows the harshest brutality on the part of the soldiers, and yet the audience does not assign final responsibility to them. Indeed, they are not finally aligned in vengeance or justice with Satan or with the temple authorities. Instead, the circling figure of Satan, always left, never right, is intercut with the livid faces of the soldiers. The cinematography implies that, unknown to them, it is Satan's power that drives them on. Pilate, in trying to reduce the severity of the scourging, represents the Roman imperial power as being concerned with justice by its own lights. He recognizes that the charges are trumped up. He tries to protect order and right. For the remainder of the movie, Rome, both as imperial power, represented by Pilate and his wife, and as a militant people, represented by the soldiers, will be shown as on the verge of belief in Jesus. By the "money shot," the final scene, there will even be converts from among the soldiers themselves. All these characters and the world structure that they represent will be drawn to the side of Jesus. Satan will receive no converts; those on his side remain on his side.

THE IMPORTANCE OF MARY THE MOTHER

No Hollywood Jesus film has ever given such significance to Mary, the mother, as does *The Passion of the Christ*. *Jesus of Nazareth* made her a model of perfect devotion and faith. *The Passion of the Christ*, particularly at the foot of the cross, references the shots of Mary developed in *Jesus of Nazareth*. Perhaps because *The Passion of the Christ* focuses on such a short time frame, Mary stands out the more. In contrast to previous Jesus films, she is shown as constantly present. Her appearance at the house of Caiaphas during and after Jesus' trial culminates with the shot of Jesus visually shown below her, confined in a dungeon beneath the pavement of the high priest's courtyard. The shot, which moves from above to below, shows the response of Jesus to her presence. Without doubt there is a specific emotional and spiritual tie. Mary becomes Jesus' partner in the Crucifixion and thereby the salvation of humanity. As the scene reveals she is a middle character on the mythic stage, found between Jesus and God.

We have already examined in part the role of Mary in the scourging scene. She has unnatural and historically implausible access to every aspect of Jesus' suffering. She mops up the blood from the scene of torture. No reason for this is given in the film; therefore, viewers must either ignore the scene or ideally supply a meaning from their own piety. Therefore, an audience "schooled" or aware of traditional Catholic contemplation of the role of the Mother sees this as the preservation of the holy blood by the Mother. Others of the audience may be confused, repulsed, or bewildered.

Why are these women cleaning up the courtyard of Pilate's headquarters? The scene dramatically functions to bring women to Mary. Magdalene has been shown as accompanying Mary throughout the film, so her presence here is unremarkable. The most unaccountable action is, however, the action of Claudia, the wife of Pilate, who has the inspiration to bring linen towels for the mopping operation. Are these women to be regarded as clean freaks? No, the scene cements a spiritual God-given connection between the three. Claudia becomes one of the believers by aligning herself with the Mother. The film goes on to portray these three and almost all other women in the movie as believers in Jesus. It establishes Mary symbolically as the precursor and mother of women converts.

At only one point does Mary waver. On the Via Dolorosa she is blocked from viewing Jesus' march toward Golgatha. She finally sees him from an alleyway. Too troubled to continue, she stops, falls against the wall, and turns away. Looking backwards, she sees Jesus fall and flashes back to Jesus falling as a toddler. Our parenthood is evoked. This is the one of the most emotional and riveting moments in the film. Her line that links the scene to the flashback is, "I'm here." Jesus' response from under the cross as he rises is, "See Mother, I make all things new." Unlike the Jesus of *The Last Temptation of Christ*, this Jesus never needs ask forgiveness from his mother. Instead, he empowers her faith. From this point on Mary never wavers. Her spirit, which has aided him through the scourging, now is unified with his in his mission of self-sacrifice. Mary becomes an intimate co-redeemer with Jesus. She and the Christ are now two parts of one act of salvation. In this way, *The Passion of the Christ* supplies a very different female side to the theological equation of salvation as compared to other Jesus films. Catholic traditional veneration of the Mother comes into full view for the first time in Hollywood history.

Other women fall into line behind Mary. In addition to Mary, Magdalene, and Claudia, the legendary character Veronica is shown wiping the fallen Jesus' face with a towel after leaving her small child in her house. This Catholic element first entered mainstream film in *King of Kings* (1961). *The Passion of the Christ*, which comes out of the tradition of *Jesus of Nazareth*, can now presume that no one in its target audience of traditionals, both Evangelicals and Catholics, will object. The moment now is filmic, not to be tested against scripture.

The careful viewer will also note a relative absence of women in the mob scenes where the angry crowd threatens revolution if Jesus is not crucified. As Jesus moves toward Golgotha, the women are those who frequently express sorrow or pity. The women express the spirit of Mary the Mother.

Mary, therefore, functions as the true believer, co-redeemer, and spiritual leader of the feminine as expressed in the film. Following an encoded form introduced by DeMille, she appears on screen in robes directly evocative of the habits worn by traditional sisters. She is thereby the Mother of the Church.

THE EXONERATION OF PILATE

No Hollywood film has ever gone to such lengths to exonerate Pilate, as the representative of the Roman imperial state, for the death of Jesus. And while each Gospel has its own account, and we should not conflate them, it is fair to say that no individual Gospel writer went to the extraordinary lengths that Gibson does to exonerate Pilate. Nor do the Gospels, taken collectively, do so. The idea that Pilate and his wife ultimately become believers is based on later Christian legend.

This being the case, we have unusually clear evidence for the director's own view. Pilate, presented with Jesus, does everything he can to release him. He resorts to the scourging as a means to persuade Caiaphas and the mob that Jesus has been punished enough. This is made apparent by the command through Abenader not to let the soldiers kill Jesus. His motivation for finally crucifying Jesus, clearly stated in the film, is that he fears an armed rebellion that would result in his recall to Rome and execution.

Pilate, along with his wife, Claudia, who is troubled in her sleep about Jesus, are shown as tender people who want to do what is right in a difficult situation. Pilate and Claudia, like the Roman soldiers, are left as potential converts. The death of Jesus is seen as a mistake of justice. Rome's power is not bad; it is simply not yet converted to the good. The mistake of justice is brought about by the unjustified threat of mob violence and rebellion against legitimate, if not well-informed, governmental authority. Hence, our sympathy is not only with Pilate but with the Roman state as well.

CAIAPHAS AND THE JEWISH AUTHORITIES

By reducing the role of Pilate and Rome, *The Passion of the Christ* focuses the audience's attention on the responsibility of the Jewish authorities. In *The Passion of the Christ* we see a reversal of the consistent Hollywood tradition of downplaying Jewish responsibility for the death of Jesus. No previous Hollywood film has pushed the line toward full frontal anti-Semitism as far as *The Passion of the Christ*. It barely maintains plausible deniability for itself and its advocates.

Jewish authorities are consistently shown as devious and manipulative. In a totally fictitious scene, Mary Magdalene begs a Roman soldier to prevent the Jewish guards from taking Jesus illegally at night into the high priest's house. A temple guard intervenes, indicating that it is a religious matter and that she is crazy. The Romans cannot maintain justice because the Jewish authorities self-consciously subvert it.

As presented in the film, the decision to condemn Jesus shows no influence by Satan. Unlike the Roman scourging or later mob scenes before Pilate, the Jewish authorities willfully condemn Jesus. While the film indicates, as do the Gospels, that false testimony is given at the interrogation at Caiaphas's house, it also chooses to have Jesus directly say that he is the Son of God. This establishes a clear basis from the perspective of Jewish law for the condemnation of Jesus. The statement is blasphemous.

By placing this interpretation directly before the viewer, *The Passion of the Christ* presents the choice: Either you believe Jesus is God's Son or you don't. This choice, in and of itself, is not anti-Semitic. Some Jews in the movie do believe in Jesus, while most do not. Rather the anti-Judaism is deployed throughout the remainder of the film along classic Christian anti-Semitic lines. That is to say, at every turn the film represents the activities of Jewish officials to coincide with later Christian rationalizations for the persecution and annihilation of the Jews. At least as early as 383 C.E., St. John Chrysostom charged the Jews with being Christ killers.

Most important for the viewer of the film is recognition of the subtlety of characterization. The alienating otherness of "the Jews" in Jesus movies has, as we have seen, been constructed in a variety of ways. But the general approach since *King of Kings* (1961) has been to eradicate any clear markers of ethnic Judaism, thereby also implying the erasure of modern Jews by American society. Where Jewish otherness is depicted and recognizable as being the most foreign to the viewer's own culture, it is applied primarily to the Jews who oppose Jesus. This otherness accords with representations of Orthodox Judaism in the American mainstream, both contemporary and medieval, and it is then placed by the films into the first century. *The Passion of the Christ* follows the established Hollywood conventions. In the same way that Mary and Magdalene are shown as visually similar to ordered Catholic sisters, the Jewish authorities look the most like stereotypes of Jews.

The film accomplishes this visually. The temple guards and the Sanhedrin have fuller beards than others. Many of them even have suggestions of traditional forelocks. The members of the Sanhedrin particularly are dressed in the costume later associated with orthodoxy. Prayer shawls are suggested. As in *Jesus of Nazareth,* the Pharisees appear at the trial and are dressed within the range of traditional Jewish garments. Although we, as audience, may know that everyone in a particular shot is Jewish, the ones who oppose Jesus conform in costume and image to the otherness that is not the American conception of Jesus and his disciples. Instead, Jesus and his followers conform to church images of Jesus. They also closely resemble images of the Jesus movie tradition.

Adding to this visual depiction of the opponents as real, other Jews is the depiction of the only other Jewish authority, Herod Antipas. Following the typology introduced by *Jesus Christ Superstar,* Herod appears as a Boy George look-alike in ill-fitting wig with painted courtesans, male and female, in attendance. The only African in the film is one of these courtesans. The scene amounts to little dramatically and seems to be added primarily to accord with the film's attempt to pour every Gospel account into its mix. As we have said elsewhere it in no way accords with historical knowledge about Herod. It reveals by its images the film's attitude toward homosexuality. Interestingly, in spite of the tradition of showing Romans as homosexual in Hollywood epics, *The Passion of the Christ* only represents a Jew in this manner. Clearly the representation is derogatory.

The Passion of the Christ shows the unrelenting opposition of the Jewish authorities. They are structured iconographically in the scourging scene. Caiaphas, as in *King of Kings* (1927), becomes the primary instrument of condemnation. Unlike the earlier movie, however, his ill will can be accounted for religiously. Jesus is genuinely a blasphemer in his eyes. Also, unlike *King of Kings* (1927), Caiaphas in *The Passion of the Christ* never repents. He is shown repeatedly in group settings as the leader of the opposition, including mob scenes where Caiaphas leads. In the mob scene before Pilate, as in *The Greatest Story Ever Told,* Satan stirs the crowd, while at the center stand Caiaphas and other authorities. By the threat of terrorism, the Jewish mob gets what it wants.

THE CRUCIFIXION AS CLIMAX

These threads—Jesus as action hero, Mary as co-redemptrix, Rome as mission field, Judaism as condemned—all come together in the final two scenes of the film: the Crucifixion and Resurrection.

Divine judgment comes at the Crucifixion. *The Passion of the Christ* breaks new territory here, departing from the Gospels and previous Jesus movies. As in any good action movie, the bad guys must be seen as judged. So we should not be surprised at the new detail that the crow introduced by DeMille pecks out the eyes of the very thief who previously disbelieved Jesus. The moral economy of the film completed in the Crucifixion scene brings it into line with the moral economy of the typical action movie.

The "tear of God" falls from the sky initiating an earthquake that shakes Jerusalem, sends a tremor through the bedroom of Pilate and Claudia, and ends by splitting the temple, the Holy of Holies, the veil, and the ark of the covenant in two. Satan is shown from a high shot, in a circle of light on a barren desert floor. Roman soldiers, responding to the earthquake, break the legs of the prisoners, but spear Jesus in the side. In a shot as strange as it is evocative, the soldier delivering the stroke falls to his knees in a position of supplication as he is literally bathed in the blood from the side of Jesus.

Who is judged? Who is saved? The central shrine of Judaism is destroyed by God at the giving up of Jesus' life. The Ark of the Covenant is literally split in two. No movie, no Gospel does this. The Romans begin the road to salvation. God's earthquake does no damage to the bedroom of Pilate and Claudia. Satan, shown from God's perspective shot in a barren circle of light on a desert floor, is defeated. Symbolically, hell is emptied. Jesus has won the wager, and God judges Satan accordingly.

The scene also provides the conclusion to the story of Mary the Mother. She receives her commission as Mother of the Beloved Disciple and thereby of the church. She adores the body as it comes down from the cross. *The Passion of the Christ* attempts both an allusion to Michelangelo's *Pieta* and more specifically to Zeffirelli's shot in *Jesus of Nazareth*. The angle, however, is off and the lighting too blue and hyperreal. Instead, we see the grotesqueness of her bloody mouth as she gazes directly into the lens of the camera.

The gaze connects her through the camera to the next scene, the Resurrection. Mary's gaze unites her with the opening of Jesus' eyes inside the tomb. Her eyes become those of the resurrecting Christ.

King of Kings (1927) presents the conversation between Magdalene and Jesus to complete the story of Magdalene and establishes her as the ideal convert. Jesus' subsequent ascension cements the bridge between the ancient story and the contemporary American aspirations for the future. *King of Kings* (1927) links the future of America directly to the past of the ascending Christ.

Unlike DeMille, Gibson provides no hope of peace for the audience. The audience is given only Jesus' view of the Resurrection, is made to identify with him, and only fleetingly allowed adoration or reflection. Instead, the position of the viewer is to follow the resurrected Lord from the tomb.

No character offers interpretation or response. Mary's gaze into the camera, which concluded the Crucifixion scene, becomes Jesus' perspective as the light slowly crosses the roof of the tomb. We see through Jesus' eyes the grave shroud deflate. Then the point of view shifts and the camera caresses Jesus, starting from the head. He is naked. He is the iconic embodiment of the perfected American male hero. The contrast to the bloody mass last seen on the cross is dramatic.

As the camera moves from head to thigh, the holes in his hands glow, martial music gathers, and we watch his thigh as he strides from the tomb. The film ends, but establishes the direction of the viewer. The underlying structure or map provided in the film, latent though it is, propels the viewer toward certain predispositions for completing the film. Here Hollywood completes its new making of the American Christ.

HOLLYWOOD'S MAKING OF THE AMERICAN CHRIST AS ACTION HERO

In order to appreciate fully the accomplishment of the film, I would point out specific film techniques that have gone into the establishing of this particular Christ. Chief among them are the use of slow motion, close-ups, and flashbacks, the combination of action epic and foreign language genre conventions, and the use of computer-generated images (CGI).

The Passion of the Christ's contributions to the tradition of the Cinematic Savior is most powerfully, perhaps most sporadically, realized by cinematic techniques that establish Jesus as the epic action hero. In terms of the tradition of Jesus movies, *The Passion of the Christ* uses the well-established technique of framing and holding shots that reference traditions of church art. In Gibson's case the referencing is clearly to Caravaggio.

The use of extensive slow motion in the scenes leading to Golgotha extends the filmic tradition introduced in *The Last Temptation of Christ.* In *The Passion of the Christ,* it becomes so predictable as to be almost boring. Slow-motion techniques are a staple of American film generally, but, especially since the work of Sam Peckinpah in *The Wild Bunch,* their use has blossomed in action films. The single most overused technique in *The Passion of the Christ* is the use of slow motion as a means of emphasizing the violent brutality done to Jesus. In addition, it seems to be a fall-back technique to enhance otherwise nonaction sequences. For example, the slow motion of the purse thrown from Caiaphas to Judas lacks any particular dramatic impact.

I have already noted the use of close-ups for establishing the mythological structure of the film. The impact of the close-up takes on additional significance in the context of the creation of an *ancient* foreign language film. Given that we are viewing a Hollywood production, this is an extremely artificial but intimately controlling directorial decision. Because Latin and Aramaic are no longer spoken extensively in the contemporary world (Latin has no living populations for whom it is a primary language; Aramaic is spoken only by very small populations located primarily in Syria and Lebanon), this film depends almost exclusively on visual narrative for communication. The movie also withholds large amounts of dialogue from the viewer by refusing to subtitle it, superficially an almost inexplicable move. For example most of the soldiers' derision during the scourging remains untitled. The interviews between Pilate, Caiaphas, and Jesus occur in both Aramaic and Latin. Notoriously, the film preserves in Aramaic the crowd saying, "His blood be on ourselves and upon our children." The line remains untitled, thereby establishing a point of plausible deniability of anti-Semitism.

By its use of language unfamiliar to the audience, the film places the viewer at the mercy of the titles for basic direction in how to understand the overt spoken narrative of the film. Ostensibly, the use of ancient languages creates an aura of "authenticity." The authenticity, however, remains more apparent than real, since Greek, not Latin, would have been the lingua franca between Roman soldiers, most of whom would have been recruited from the eastern Mediterranean basin and would speak little or no Latin. In this case, then, the Gospels' use of Greek (not Aramaic or Latin) would more closely reflect the realities of interaction with Pilate.

The final, latent, but no less important effect of using Latin and Aramaic in the film is that it structures the more familiar tones and syntax of Romance languages based on Latin in opposition to the Semitic of Aramaic. To the untrained ear, Aramaic sounds very close to Arabic. Hence, the future mission field of the Roman West is indicated against the past of Jewish rejection. More importantly, the current perceived threat from Semitic speakers (Arabic) underlies the viewer's rejection of the Jewish population as a terroristic force against the civilized-sounding Romans (notably here *not* employing suspect British accents). Jesus operates in the scene with Pilate as a bridge figure who speaks both his native Aramaic and (Romance) Latin. Satan, we should note, only speaks Aramaic.

Audience formation and reception is of course a difficult issue in film analysis, marked as it is by insecurity with regard to historical audiences—which is a complex way of asking why the film's preferences are what they are. What this film suggests by its use of the two specific ancient languages is that the future of Christianity lies in the direction of Rome, Western Europe, and ultimately the Americas. Without recourse to East Coast and upper-class British accents, it substantiates the characterization of the Romans, Jesus, and his followers as most like contemporary Americans, and instantiates the characterization of Satan and the Jews as least like us. The threat to America, the film implies, is from Arabic peoples. The move is but a small jump from filmic culture to post-9/11 America.

Interesting, too, is that *The Passion of the Christ* extensively uses the technique of flashback to refer the audience to earlier scenes in the life of Jesus. Rather than as an opportunity to bring in such crucial parts of the Jesus story as the parables, the miracles and the teaching, however, these early scenes are domestic and serve to establish the all-important tie between Mary and Jesus. They are fictive and noncanonical. Most artistically, and most fictively as in earlier Jesus movies, the scenes with Mary develop the household life of Jesus. There is the humorous scene of creating a modern dining table for a rich man. Mary's connection with Jesus establishes his humanity, his beauty, and the emotional basis for their unified spirits in the Passion.

Later, scenes derived from the Gospels, particularly the Last Supper in John, predominate, especially during the Crucifixion. The Crucifixion becomes the enactment of the elements of the Supper, with strong emphasis on the element of the Christ's blood. In addition the suffering and coming persecution of Jesus' disciples are integrated with the interpretation of Jesus' body and blood. In this *The Passion of the Christ* develops a sacramentality similar to that of *Jesus of Nazareth* and *The Last Temptation of Christ*.

Most strikingly, *The Passion of the Christ* incorporates the use of computer-generated images, now a staple of epic and action films, but unavailable to a previous generation of Jesus-movie makers. *The Passion of the Christ* uses the technique almost exclusively to depict the supernatural realm. Most noteworthy are the two final scenes. The tear of God that initiates the judgment sequence jars by its contrast with the overall tonality of the film. This is paralleled by the high shot of Satan alone in hell. In these cases the CGI fails to create a seamless shift from history to myth. What results is an emotional distancing of the viewer who perceives too readily that we have now entered not theological or sacred but rather hyper real space. This has most to do with color palette, which as we saw in the last chapter has been borrowed from realistic and sci-fi film styles. It also has to do with the blatant exposure in these scenes of the hyperreality of the film itself. Such a look also carries over into the Resurrection scene, especially in the enhancement of the scarred hands. It remains of a piece with the brief glimpse of the world of evil given in the externalization of Judas's evil, green, ghoulish spirit earlier in the film in the scene of his confrontation with Jesus beneath the bridge. The use of CGI in this way has more to do with the horror movie genre than with the traditions of Jesus movies. It also reveals a continuing discomfort with the transcendent realm that was noticeable in modern Jesus movies such as *The Greatest Story Ever Told*. Despite its pretensions to piety, *The Passion of the Christ* remains exceptionally uncomfortable about God.

The combination of action movie genre and epic movie conceits with the traditional Hollywood Jesus movie elements results in a new Christ who is best characterized as a media-created hyperreality. Designating this Christ is the color of the film, which is dominated once again by the blue tone used by *The Matrix, AI, Minority Report* and others. It also references the use of grainy blue as an homage to the film noir style of *Payback* and other movies in that genre. A further indexing of film palettes currently in use in Hollywood indicates that genres are falling into certain color schemes to indicate their realities. Hence red moves toward the surreal world, blue hyperreal, yellow romantic. In each case, the choice of palette, in combination with plot and characterization, designates a desired level of viewer predisposition. By the choice of blue, *The Passion of the Christ* heightens viewer anticipation and predilection for seeing the film by absorbing it into the mythic expectation of the epic/action hero genre. The palette also suggests that the audience is seeing the truly real mythic and dystopian structure of the world. The common thread of dread and anxiety that connects the ancient scene to the contemporary is exposed.

The absorption of the Jesus movie into the action hero genre means that the film naturally and necessarily divides the world into a conflict between good and evil. The hero triumphs, and is supposed by the viewer to continue to triumph off screen or, as we have seen in *Shane, High Plains Drifter*, and *Pale Rider*, to ride off to resurrection and revenge another day. In *The Passion of the Christ*, the viewer arrives at the final scene with these sensibilities heightened by the entire film.

Those who believed in Jesus, Mary, Magdalene, and the disciples adopt the preferred and good perspective to which the viewer is also called. They express piety, faith, and family values. The Romans, representing secular governmental power, are on the verge of salvation. The opponents are other. They are less attractive, even ugly, more Semitic, and not in any way seen as Western European or American. They connive and resort to terrorist tactics to gain their objectives. They persecute the truth. And this whole structure in its full exposure of hyperreality, the more real than real, reveals current American life.

In the post-9/11 world, the myth of the film comes into strong focus. A core of true Christian believers must convert the secular state to Christ and Christian values. This will save us from the "Jew" within who stands in as a code designation of liberals, gays, and all those who oppose Christian American values. By becoming strong in this way we will also be able to resist the onset of Semitic foreigners who wish to destroy our culture through mob violence and terror. The American Christ at the end of the movie strides forward to battle. The message is convert, be forgiven, or be judged. As Jack Graham, President of the Southern Baptist Convention, said, "This is a providence of God, that in the midst of an international war on terrorism, in the midst of a cultural and domestic war for the family, God raises up a standard."[1] Graham is not simply using a movie as an occasion to express a militant Evangelical perspective; he has read the film correctly. The film indicates a militant, action-oriented and Christian America faced with rot and subversion from within and terrorism from without. Hence, Caiaphas and defunct Judaism along with the gay Herod represent those on the "left" who subvert the true nature of Christian America and seek to misuse the government to bring about their desires.

The Romans indicate the secular American government now on the verge of conversion. The threat of international terrorism is implied by the mob's threat of rebellion led by Caiaphas. This is not an allegory, but an unmistakable mythic structure.

Film's language is image. In mainstream movies Jesus seldom dies for our sins. The only tie to our sins in *The Passion of the Christ* is the opening title from Isaiah 53. Visually Jesus dies overwhelmed by sinners who are not us, who crave power, false religion, and the destabilization of legitimate government. The film regards Jesus as us. *The Passion of the Christ* leads us naturally into the supposition that they did it. We do not see ourselves as symbolically, or metaphorically, responsible for the death of Jesus. Real, true, Christian America would never kill Jesus. In this conclusion, as in previous chapters, I strive for an interpretation generated by the film itself. I am not concerned with the director's intention, his disclaimers, or the disclaimers of others.

Therefore, the coalition of traditionals, Catholics and Evangelicals, that compose one stream of the interpretation of Jesus in Hollywood film see this movie as spiritually uplifting. They also are appreciating a particular vision of a purified Christian America by adopting this new Cinematic Savior as their own American Christ. Compared to *King of Kings* (1927), *The Passion of the Christ* capitalizes on the biblical illiteracy of postmodern Evangelicals and Catholics. Authenticity becomes a marketing device, not a description of content. Evangelicals accept the hyperreality of the film because it placards the horrors of Crucifixion in much the same terms as did evangelistic preaching for conversion during the twentieth century. Such preaching emphasizes the sentimental tie between the emotive and the spiritual. Catholic traditionalists see their own piety fully displayed on screen, especially with regards to the role of the Virgin Mother in redemption. From either traditionalist perspective, the hope for this film remains in the conversion of the world to the American project presided over by the American Christ who embodies our values.

Thoroughly compatible with such hope, the adoption of the action movie genre to the Jesus story necessitates a thorough structuring of the film world into for or against, good versus evil. Jesus becomes the American action hero carrying with him the expectation of such heroes who always suffer silently and triumph in the end. The lack of subtlety demanded by the genre results in an unnatural narrowing of the myth of Christ. In that myth as told in the Gospels, the classic dualities of death and life are overcome and reconfigured by Jesus' Crucifixion and Resurrection. A universality is thereby introduced that refuses a division of the world or nation into them and us, because all live and all die, all crucify and are crucified, all are resurrected. *The Passion of the Christ* entraps the audience in a mythic cycle of death–conversion. It truncates and reduces the Christ myth into an instrument of political power over others rather than eternal life through resurrection for all. To the extent that *The Passion of the Christ* calls forth images of Christ as standard-bearers for war, it places our real world at risk, once again, of imperialistic violence in the name of the Prince of Peace.

CONCLUSION: WHERE DOES JESUS LEAD US?

The Cinematic Savior and the American Christ presented in Gibson's *The Passion of the Christ* bring us full circle and return us to the Christ resurrected over America 77 years earlier in DeMille's *King of Kings*. But along the pathway of his Hollywood making and remaking, he has lost some traits and gained others. It would be elegant and pleasant for a book of this sort to offer sound bites to portray an upward evolution of the Cinematic Savior, because if that were the case, we could be at least heartened by the knowledge that the projected American Christ of Hollywood might well coincide with our evolution as a nation. Unfortunately, the previous chapters have shown that easy conclusions about Hollywood's making of the American Christ are no more available to us than are similarly satisfying conclusions about the culture he represents.

If it were the case that we could easily see how the liberal, left-leaning Hollywood establishment has robbed us of our identity, then we all could join with those who would demonize Hollywood and its values as contrary to some true, persecuted Christian American spirit. Conversely, if Hollywood were the veiled mouthpiece for a right-wing conspiracy against freedom to seek out individual answers to ultimate questions of our role in the universe and world, then we could all rise up in alarm at the suppression being enacted upon us. Neither Hollywood, nor its Cinematic Savior, is at either extreme.

Instead, a complex set of images, themes, motifs, and meanings emerge. When he is present, the Cinematic Savior is a complex symbol, an identity informed by the whole of the Hollywood film history and the religious views of the audience to which those films are marketed. He now is a consumer product, an icon, both in the sense of a traditional religious object worthy of worship and in the sense of a recent advertisement for Ford's Mustang: "An American Icon of Performance and Style."

We have seen Jesus move from the rather peaceful and passive Sunday school image of DeMille's vision to Ray's New Man, Messiah of Peace. He has been refashioned as an ethereal, otherworldly presence in Stevens' depiction of the Logos of God calling us to a new evolutionary jump of inward spirituality. He has become a tired, all-too-human common man beset by existential crisis in Jewison's *Jesus Christ Superstar* before being portrayed as a man in deep psychological turmoil in Scorsese's *The Last Temptation of Christ*. Our last riveting glimpse of him is of his perfected humanity striding confidently with divine approval into the world, fresh from Resurrection and carrying with him the promise of judgment and justice. And he will reappear again, probably sooner rather than later, refashioned if not as Jesus himself, then as some other character who bears with him the meanings so well established for Jesus by Hollywood tradition.

Jesus has become the bearer of America, reflecting certainty, anxiety, alienation, and self-assurance. As surely as he is projected as screen presence, he is projected as us. The general run of the tradition out of Hollywood has been to make him into an embodiment of our national aspirations, values, even our myths about ourselves. Even *Jesus Christ Superstar* and *The Last Temptation of Christ*, where he is most human, most in conflict, presume for their effect an underlying American consensus that Jesus is ours, and is recognizable in our own reality. With *Jesus Christ Superstar* Jesus finally becomes a true American hero who faces our real doubts and willingly accepts what he does not understand. This reality now has become the bedrock of film treatment of Jesus. Even *The Passion of the Christ*, whose theology could not be more different from that of *Jesus Christ Superstar*, begins with the wager between Satan and Jesus: No one has ever been able to accept the sins of the world.

Because Hollywood myths are at root American and Christian, there is little evidence of a discreet style for treating Jesus in its film. The same techniques have been used to depict Jesus as those used for any other American hero. So far as Hollywood is concerned, the supposed division between secular and religious America is a false one. The battle over these films and others in the culture wars is not a war of cultures but a war within a culture. The battle is over mythic polarities and their resolution into the norms of a single, American Christian culture.

There are distinct shifts in style and presentation, however, that have led us to the current Cinematic Savior. The growing discomfort with the modern Protestant mainstream, reflected in the clean, modern styles of Ray and Stevens, gives way to the exploration of a more tradition-ally Catholic sacramental world from *Jesus Christ Superstar* onward. This change matches one that can be seen in other genres of Hollywood film since 1968, beginning with a comparison of the works of Kubrick (*2001: A Space Odyssey*) and Polanski (*Rosemary's Baby*). It represents an over-turning of the modern consensus that the supernatural is largely absent from the current world in favor of a more traditional view that sees the supernatural as integrated, if hidden, within the world.

It will come as no surprise to students of American religion that the Cinematic Savior consistently represents an inner spirituality: the conver-sion of the individual as the solution to the broader problems of society. Almost exclusively, with the possible exception of *Jesus Christ Superstar*, Jesus represents middle-class American values, shaping them to Cold War necessities, or the shift to suburbia.

More surprising is that Hollywood felt early on the development of two market audiences: non-traditional spiritual seekers and traditionals who are largely Evangelical and Catholic. *Jesus Christ Superstar*, *The Last Temp-tation of Christ*, *Jesus of Nazareth*, and *The Passion of the Christ* address one or the other of these markets. The current horizon of religiously themed films released or under production (*The Chronicles of Narnia* [2005] and *The Da Vinci Code* [2006]) shows no change in this market strategy.

The last three Jesus movies rely on the affirmation taken from Isaiah 53, that the Messiah suffers for our sins, as the climactic theology through which we are to understand the Crucifixion of Jesus. This new element introduced by three Catholic directors (Zeffirelli, Scorsese, and Gibson) becomes graphically dominant in *The Passion of the Christ*, where it is linked directly and visually to God's judgment against evil and sinners. In this, *The Passion of the Christ* reverses earlier representations of the Crucifixion as the point of the descent of God's mercy, indicated in *The Greatest Story Ever Told* and *Jesus of Nazareth* by a healing rain. DeMille had provided the theme of judgment in *King of Kings* (1927), yet one more of the simi-larities between the two films that we noted early on in this study, but until *The Passion of the Christ*, judgment (and retribution) had largely disappeared.

The focus on Jesus as a suffering messiah steadily allowed for a more complete fulfillment of DeMille's formula of sex, sadism, and melodrama. In this dominant Hollywood approach, Mary Magdalene becomes the focus of sexual interest for the viewer or, as in *The Last Temptation of*

Christ, for Jesus himself. In this last movie we have the suggestion, based on Christian legendary material, that Jesus survived the cross and fathered children with Mary. *The Da Vinci Code* will make this supposition, this alternative history, into the basis of its intrigue.

Sadism becomes increasingly linked to sexuality, whether in the homo-sexual depiction of Herod Antipas or Pilate, beginning with *Jesus Christ Superstar*, or through the primitive sexual dominance of the Roman soldiers at the scourging in *The Passion of the Christ*. The theology of Isaiah 53 remains largely represented on film, nevertheless. For in regard to the biblical text the traditional Christian interpretation emphasizes that Jesus dies for our sins. We have been unable to discover a movie that convincingly shows us how Jesus dies for our sins. They are usually the sins of others.

Melodrama is enhanced throughout the Hollywood tradition, especially by the steady elevation of Judas to heroic status almost equal to Jesus. This fascination with Judas, who at the beginning of the tradition—in *King of Kings* (1927)—represents the drive of greed and political power, gives way to various accounts of Judas until in *The Last Temptation of Christ* he becomes the best friend of Jesus who does not betray but enables the saving sacrifice. The return, in *The Passion of the Christ*, to a rather more traditional interpretation of Judas (he succumbed to possession by Satan) notwithstanding, the Hollywood tradition of Judas indicates a continuing American fascination with the quintessential character of betrayal in Western culture. Our uneasiness with Judas reflects perhaps our own suspicion that we, collectively, have also betrayed.

Judas is also frequently aligned with Jewish unbelief in the story of Jesus. While Hollywood, until the notable reversion in *The Passion of the Christ*, shows a consistent sensitivity to the problem of anti-Semitism, it nevertheless also shows Christianity to be the true religion that displaces the old, defunct religion of the Jews. Except in *Jesus Christ Superstar* and *The Last Temptation of Christ*, this view of Christian successionism recurs in various forms. *The Passion of the Christ* reverses the Hollywood tradition and constructs the Jews as hostile other who are responsible for the death of Jesus, and are judged for it.

Women in the Hollywood tradition of the Cinematic Savior seldom rise above dichotomized stereotypes of the evil woman as licentious temptress and the good woman as devout wife and mother, confined to the domestic realm. The exception is Magdalene in *Jesus Christ Superstar*, who emerges as a fully complex character. Remarkably for the time, Magdalene in DeMille's depiction already showed signs of character development (in a silent film no less) that promised some move beyond simple stereotype.

Although she is absorbed into the household by her dress, she is made into the ultimate faithful disciple of Jesus by her conversion, presence at the cross, and visit to the tomb. She embodies the contemplation by the soul of divine truth.

Here I must also state an admiration for the powerful depiction of Mary the mother in *The Passion of the Christ*. Whatever we may think of her elevation in this movie to the status of co-redemptrix with Jesus, she expresses a determined spirituality and is able to give us the most compelling dramatic representation of Mary in film. Protestant mainstream film treatments have shied away from such an elevation of the figure, but interestingly enough it appears to have provoked little discomfort from Protestant supporters of *The Passion of the Christ*.

Romans more often than not exist primarily as an undeveloped backdrop to the story of Jesus, except where they emerge as the potential field of Christian mission as in *Jesus of Nazareth* and especially *The Passion of the Christ*. They stand in for various forms of political authoritarianism, usually international threats to America, either past (the British) or present (the Soviet Union as in *King of Kings* [1961]). Where they are to be seen as America, they represent the unconverted, frequently governmental element of American society. Therefore, when seen from the perspective of the Hollywood tradition, Gibson's altogether sympathetic treatment of Pilate should come as no surprise. As in so much else, however, this summary does not capture the nuances that we have witnessed in the detailed analysis of each movie.

The surprising insight that comes from this discussion and comparison has been that by a series of short sidesteps the Cinematic Savior has steadily taken on the full arsenal of the American action hero. The ability of Hollywood to adapt the action heroes of epics, Westerns, Sci-Fi, and even film noir to the Jesus story was not something I anticipated as I began my work. That those elements would then come to the fore in the most recent Jesus movie came as a shock.

Of course the precursors were there. In every movie up until *Jesus Christ Superstar*, Jesus, while interesting and of course worthy, never achieved the dramatic heroic thrill of other movie characters. The Superman, Wyatt Earp, and Tarzan of my childhood have always held more interest for me. With the study of Jesus as a human most powerfully developed in *Jesus Christ Superstar* and *The Last Temptation of Christ*, however, Jesus himself as a model for heroic action took on considerable interest, even though his depiction in such a way overturned more traditional theological views. Most importantly these two films do not adopt the standard epic model that otherwise dominates the Jesus film tradition.

The necessity for America to identify with, cast itself as, and become a hero in its own view underlies this development. In *The Passion of the Christ* America's preferred view of itself as a suffering hero dominates the portrayal of the Cinematic Savior. Jesus has been mythologized anew as American action hero who leads us forth against America's enemies within her and outside her. This new form of the Cinematic Savior denotes an America that desires to be the Christian nation of what it supposes to be God's purposes.

The question that I am left with, that we are left with, is where is the real Jesus? For Hollywood, he is no longer to be found in the Gospel tradition. That was all right then, but this is now. We seem to desire a new kind of more heroic and simultaneously more reassuring Savior. Hollywood certainly seems willing to create and to market him to us. And here, we have lost those limits and questions posed by the individual Gospel portraits of Jesus that have from time to time ameliorated the tendency of all readers, the faithful and the not-so faithful, to see in him what they want to see.

The creative fictionalization of individual directors has combined with the drive of Hollywood to market its product in ways that effectively eliminate any sense of the sacred otherness of Jesus himself. One important function throughout world religions of prophets, founders, or saviors has been to critique us, our national or individual desires, and to make us rethink our role in the world both individually and collectively. When a nation considers its idealized self to be a surpassing transcendent value, it has opted out of compassionate struggle in the world. My suspicion and hope is that the real Jesus still lurks somewhere nagging at our own pride, ambitions, and aspirations.

NOTES

INTRODUCTION

1. Peter Fraser, *Images of the Passion: The Sacramental Mode in Film* (Westport, CT: Praeger Publishers, 1998); Gerald Forshey, *American Religious and Biblical Spectaculars* (Westport, CT: Praeger Publishers, 1992); Stephen Prothero, *American Jesus: How the Son of God Became a National Icon* (New York: Farrar, Straus and Giroux, 2003).

CHAPTER 1

1. Richard Stern, Clayton Jefford, and Guerric DeBona, *Savior on the Silver Screen* (New York: Paulist Press, 1999), 32.

2. Gerald Forshey, *American Religious and Biblical Spectaculars* (Westport, CT: Praeger Publishers, 1992), 16.

3. Anton Karl Kozlovic, "The Deep Focus Typecasting of Joseph Schildkraut as Judas Figure in Four DeMille Films," *Journal of Religion and Popular Culture* 4 (Spring 2004), http://www.usask.ca/relst/jrpc/art6-schildkraut.html.

4. Stern, Jefford, DeBona, 47–48.

CHAPTER 2

1. Gerald Forshey, *American Religious and Biblical Spectaculars* (Westport, CT: Praeger Publishers, 1992), 91.

2. See Janice Capel Anderson, "Feminist Criticism: The 'Dancing Daughter,'" *Mark and Method*, eds. Janice Capel Anderson and Stephen D. Moore (Minneapolis: Fortress Press, 1992), 103–134.

3. Bruce Babbington and Peter William Evans, *Biblical Epics: Sacred Narrative in the Hollywood Cinema* (Manchester, UK: Manchester University Press, 1993), 31.

4. W. Barnes Tatum, *Jesus at the Movies: A Guide to the First Hundred Years* (Santa Rosa, CA: Polebridge Press, 1997), 75.

5. Tatum, 36.

6. Forshey, 29, 91.

7. Susan Bordo, *The Male Body: A New Look At Men in Public and in Private* (New York: Farrar, Straus and Giroux, 1999), 107–82.

CHAPTER 3

1. Gerald Forshey, *American Religious and Biblical Spectaculars* (Westport, CT: Praeger Publishers, 1992), 95; Richard Stern, Clayton Jefford, and Guerric DeBona, *Savior on the Silver Screen* (New York: Paulist Press, 1999), 131.

2. Stern, Jefford, and DeBona, 147.

3. Forshey, 100.

4. Forshey, 95.

5. Forshey, 95.

CHAPTER 4

1. Gerald Forshey, *American Religious and Biblical Spectaculars* (Westport, CT: Praeger Publishers, 1992), 109.

2. Compare my use of "sacramental" here with that of Peter Fraser, *Images of the Passion: The Sacramental Mode in Film* (Westport, CT: Praeger Publishers, 1998).

3. Michael Wood, *America at the Movies or "Santa Maria, It Had Slipped My Mind"* (New York: Basic Books, 1975), 135–45.

4. Tom Wolfe, *The Electric Kool-Aid Acid Test* (New York: Bantam Books, 1999 [c.1968]).

CHAPTER 5

1. In 1979 an additional three hours were added to a new edition. Here I will deal only with the original, shorter version.

2. W. Barnes Tatum, *Jesus at the Movies: A Guide to the First Hundred Years* (Santa Rosa, CA: Polebridge Press, 1997), 140, 145.

3. Tatum, 75.

4. Tatum, 135–36.

5. Tatum, 142.

6. Lloyd Baugh, *Imaging the Divine: Jesus and Christ-Figures in Film* (Kansas City: Sheed and Ward, 1997), 80–82.

7. Tatum, 141, offers a good review of New Testament scholarship on the suffering servant of Isaiah.

8. Baugh, 73.

9. Baugh, 79.

10. Tatum, 144.

CHAPTER 6

1. See W. Barnes Tatum, *Jesus at the Movies: A Guide to the First Hundred Years* (Santa Rosa, CA: Polebridge Press, 1997), 179–81, for a brief synopsis.

2. Richard Stern, Clayton Jefford, and Guerric DeBona, *Savior on the Silver Screen* (New York: Paulist Press, 1999), 288–91.

CHAPTER 7

1. Peter Fraser, *Images of the Passion: The Sacramental Mode in Film* (Westport, CT: Praeger Publishers, 1998), 169.

CHAPTER 8

1. David Gates, "Jesus Christ Movie Star," *Newsweek* (March 28, 2004): 50.

FILMOGRAPHY

Films are listed alphabetically by title, followed by director, principal production company, and year of first release.

A Clockwork Orange. Stanley Kubrick. Warner Brothers, 1971.
A Fist Full of Dollars. Sergio Leone. Constantin Film Produktion GmbH, 1964.
A Streetcar Named Desire. Elia Kazan. Warner Brothers, 1951.
AI. Steven Spielberg. Warner Brothers, 2001.
Apocalypse Now. Francis Ford Coppola. Zoetrope, 1979.
Ben Hur. William Wyler. MGM, 1959.
Blade Runner. Ridley Scott. Blade Runner Partnership, 1982.
Bonnie and Clyde. Arthur Penn. Warner Brothers/Seven Arts, 1967.
Braveheart. Mel Gibson. 20th Century Fox, 1995.
Brother Sun, Sister Moon. Franco Zeffirelli. Euro International Film S.p.A., 1972.
Cleopatra. Joseph L. Mankiewicz 20th Century Fox, 1963.
El Cid. Anthony Mann. Samuel Bronston Productions, 1961.
Equus. Sidney Lumet. Persky-Bright Productions, 1977.
For a Few Dollars More. Sergio Leone. Arturo Gonzales Producciones Cinematograficas S.A., 1965.
Gallipoli. Peter Weir. Australian Film Commission, 1981.
Gladiator. Ridley Scott. Dream Works SKG, 2000.
Hamlet. Franco Zeffirelli. Icon Entertainment International, 1990.
High Plains Drifter. Clint Eastwood. Malpaso Company, 1973.
Intolerance: Love's Struggle Through the Ages, D.W. Griffith, Triagle Film Corporation, 1916.
Jesus Christ Superstar. Norman Jewison. Universal Studios, 1973.

Jesus of Nazareth. Franco Zeffirelli. Incorporated Television Company, 1977.

Judgment at Nuremberg. Stanley Kramer. Roxlom Films Inc., 1961.

King of Kings. Cecil B. DeMille. Pathé Exchange Inc., 1927.

King of Kings. Nicholas Ray. Samuel Bronston Productions, 1961.

Lethal Weapon. Richard Donner. Warner Brothers, 1987.

Lethal Weapon 2. Richard Donner. Silver Pictures, 1989.

Lethal Weapon 3. Richard Donner. Silver Pictures, 1992.

Lethal Weapon 4. Richard Donner. Donner/Shuler-Donner Productions, 1998.

Mad Max. George Miller. Mad Max Films, 1979.

Mad Max 2. George Miller. Kennedy Miller Productions, 1981.

Mad Max Beyond Thunderdome. George Miller and George Ogilvie. Kennedy Miller Productions, 1985.

Minority Report. Steven Spielberg. DreamWorks SKG, 2002.

On the Waterfront. Elia Kazan. Columbia Pictures, 1954.

Pale Rider. Clint Eastwood. Malpaso, 1985.

Patriot. Roland Emmerich. Columbia Pictures, 2000.

Payback. Brian Helgeland. Icon Entertainment International, 1999.

Quo Vadis. Mervyn LeRoy. MGM, 1951.

Rebel Without a Cause. Nicholas Ray. Warner Bros, 1955.

Romeo and Juliet. Franco Zeffirelli. Dino de Laurentiis Cinematografica, 1968.

Shane. George Stevens. Paramount Pictures, 1953.

Sherlock Jr. Buster Keaton. Buster Keaton Productions, 1924.

Spartacus. Stanley Kubrick. Bryna Productions, 1960.

Star Wars. George Lucas. Lucasfilm Ltd., 1977.

Taxi Driver. Martin Scorsese. Columbia Pictures, 1976.

The Day the Earth Stood Still. Robert Wise. 20th Century Fox, 1951.

The Greatest Story Ever Told. George Stevens. United Artists, 1965.

The Jazz Singer. Alan Crosland. Warner Brothers, 1927.

The Last Temptation of Christ. Martin Scorsese. Universal Studios, 1988.

The Lord of the Rings: The Fellowship of the Ring. Peter Jackson. New Line Cinema, 2001.

The Matrix. Andy and Larry Wachowski. Village Roadshow Pictures, 1999.

The Matrix Reloaded. Andy and Larry Wachowski. Warner Brothers, 2003.

The Matrix Revolutions. Andy and Larry Wachowski. Warner Brothers, 2003.

The Passion of the Christ. Mel Gibson. Icon Productions, 2004.

The Petrified Forest. Archie Mayo. Warner Brothers, 1936.

The Sign of the Cross. Cecil B. DeMille. Paramount Publix Corporation, 1932.

The Ten Commandments. Cecil B. DeMille. Paramount Pictures, 1956.

The Unforgiven. Clint Eastwood. Malpaso Productions, 1992.

The Wild Bunch. Sam Peckinpah. Warner Brothers/Seven Arts, 1969.

Troy. Wolfgang Petersen. Warner Brothers, 2004.

Vangelo secondo Matteo (The Gospel of Matthew). Pier Paolo Passolini. Arco Film S.r.L, 1964.

Wings. William A. Wellman. Paramount Famous Lasky Corporation, 1927.

WORKS CONSULTED

Aichele, George and Richard Walsh, eds. *Screening Scripture: Intertextual Connections Between Scripture and Film*. Harrisburg, PA: Trinity Press International, 2002.

Anderson, Janice Capel. "Feminist Criticism: The 'Dancing Daughter.'" In *Mark and Method*, eds. Janice Capel Anderson and Stephen D. Moore. Minneapolis: Fortress Press, 1992.

Babbington, Bruce and Peter William Evans. *Biblical Epics: Sacred Narrative in the Hollywood Cinema*. Manchester, UK: Manchester University Press, 1993.

Baston, Bruce. *The Man Nobody Knows*, New York: Collien Books 1987 (c. 1925).

Baugh, Lloyd. *Imaging the Divine: Jesus and Christ-Figures in Film*. Kansas City: Sheed and Ward, 1997.

———. "Palestinian Braveheart: The Atonement Theology of Mel Gibson's 'Passion.'" *America* (February 23, 2004): 17–21.

Bordo, Susan. *The Male Body: A New Look At Men in Public and in Private*. New York: Farrar, Straus and Giroux, 1999.

Cecil B. DeMille: American Epic. Directed by Kevin Brownlow. Television Broadcast. Turner Classic Movies, 2004.

Forshey, Gerald. *American Religious and Biblical Spectaculars*. Media and Society Series, ed. J. Fred MacDonald. Westport, CT: Praeger Publishers, 1992.

Fraser, Peter. *Images of the Passion: The Sacramental Mode in Film*. Westport, CT: Praeger Publishers, 1998.

Gates, David. "Jesus Christ, Movie Star." *Newsweek* (March 28, 2004): 50.

Grier, Patricia. *American Jesus: Visions and Interpretations of the Gospels in American Film 1927–1988*. BA Honors thesis, Smith College, Northampton, MA, 2001.

Haskins, Susan. *Mary Magdalen: Myth and Metaphor*. New York: Harcourt Brace, 1993.

Jarnagin, Elizabeth. *Lights, Camera, Salvation! Exploring Cinematic Portrayals of Jesus Christ*. Master's thesis, The Episcopal Theological Seminary of the Southwest, Austin, TX, 2000.

Kennedy, Tammie. "(Re)Presenting Mary Magdalene: A Feminist Reading of *The Last Temptation of Christ*." *Journal of Religion and Popular Culture* 9 (Spring 2005), http://www.usask.ca/relst/jrpc/art9-scorsesemisogynist-print.html.

Klassen, William. *Judas: Betrayer or Friend of Jesus?* Minneapolis: Fortress Press, 1996.

Kozlovic, Anton Karl. "The Deep Focus Typecasting of Joseph Schildkraut as Judas Figure in Four DeMille Films." *Journal of Religion and Popular Culture* 4 (Spring 2004), http://www.usask.ca/relst/jrpc/art6-schildkraut.html.

Kraemer, Christine Hoff. "Wrestling with Flesh, Wrestling with Spirit: The Painful Consequences of Dualism in *The Last Temptation of Christ*." *Journal of Religion and Popular Culture* 8 (Fall 2004), http www.usask.ca/relst/jrpc/art8-lasttemptation-print.html.

Langenhorst, Georg. *Jesus Ging Nach Hollywood: Die Wiederentdeckung Jesu in Literatur und Film der Gägenwart*. Düsseldorf: Patmos Verlag, 1998.

Lyden, John C. *Film as Religion: Myths, Morals, and Rituals*. New York: New York University Press, 2003.

Miles, Margaret. *Seeing and Believing: Religion and Values in the Movies*. Boston: Beacon Press, 1996.

Mirimax Film Corporation. *Perspectives on the Passion of the Christ: Religious Thinkers and Writers Explore the Issues Raised by the Controversial Movie*. New York: Miramax Books, 2004.

Noah, Sara. "Historical Figures in Film: The Celluloid Christ." Master's thesis, San Jose State University, San Jose, CA, 1993.

Poland, Larry W. *The Last Temptation of Hollywood*. Highland, CA: Mastermedia International, Inc., 1988.

Prothero, Stephen. *American Jesus: How the Son of God Became a National Icon*. New York: Farrar, Straus and Giroux, 2003.

Scott, Bernard Brandon. *Hollywood Dreams and Biblical Stories*. Minneapolis: Fortress Press, 1994.

Shilling, Kaile. "Servant of the Story: Judas as Tragic Hero in Film." *The Journal of Religion and Film* 8, No. 2 (October, 2004), http://www.unomaha.edu/jrf/Vol8No2/servant.htm.

Stern, Richard, Clayton Jefford, and Guerric DeBona. *Savior on the Silver Screen*. New York: Paulist Press, 1999.

Stone, Bryan P. *Faith and Film: Theological Themes at the Cinema*. St. Louis: Chalice Press, 2000.

Tatum, W. Barnes. *Jesus at the Movies: A Guide to the First Hundred Years*. Santa Rosa, CA: Polebridge Press, 1997.

Walsh, Richard. *Reading the Gospels in the Dark: Portrayals of Jesus in Film*. New York: Trinity Press International, 2003.

Wolfe, Tom. *The Electric Kool-Aid Acid Test*. New York: Bantam Books, 1999 [c.1968]).

Wood, Michael. *America at the Movies or "Santa Maria, It Had Slipped My Mind."* New York: Basic Books, 1975.

INDEX

About the Author

STEPHENSON HUMPHRIES-BROOKS is Associate Professor of Religious Studies at Hamilton College, where he teaches courses in film, religion, and popular culture. He has been interviewed frequently on the subject of Jesus in film for outlets including the *New York Times* and NPR. He has also contributed to a number of edited collections.